D0615204

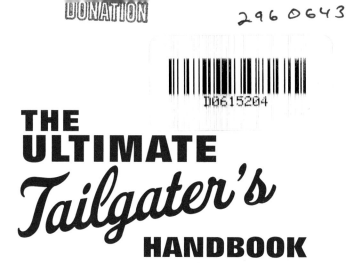

THE ULTIMATE
Tailgater's
HANDBOOK

Edited by Stephen Linn

[interactive blvd]™

An Interactive Blvd Book
www.interactiveblvd.com

RUTLEDGE HILL PRESS®

Nashville, Tennessee
A Division of Thomas Nelson Publishers
www.thomasnelson.com

www.theultimatetailgater.com

An Interactive Blvd Book. Interactive Blvd is a division of 4964 Productions, LLC, www.interactiveblvd.com.

Published by Rutledge Hill Press, a Division of Thomas Nelson, Inc., P.O. Box 141000, Nashville, Tennessee 37214.

Rutledge Hill Press books may be purchased in bulk for educational, business, fundraising, or sales promotional use. For information, please e-mail SpecialMarkets@ThomasNelson.com.

Editor: Stephen Linn
Editorial contributors: John Glass, Kate Glass, Stephen Linn, Steve Ney
Illustrations: DJ Smith
Photography: Bruce Newman (pages 12, 24, 26, 47, 122, 132, 134, 155),
Athlon Sports (pages 7, 8, 9, 16, 27, 66, 105, 106, 109, 153), David Bailey (page 97),
Brian Spurlock/Sportchrome (page 89), Rob Tringali/Sportschrome (pages 42, 71, 83),
Nashville Sports Council (pages 32, 215, 217), all others Ed Rode
Recipes on pages 101, 106, 111, 113, 115 courtesy of Joe Cahn, Commissioner of Tailgating
Design: Creative Access, Inc., Nashville, Tennessee

Library of Congress Cataloging-in-Publication Data

Linn, Stephen, 1964–
  The ultimate tailgater's handbook / edited by Stephen Linn.
    p. cm. — (Interactive Blvd book)
  "An Interactive Blvd Book."
  ISBN 1-4016-0224-X (pbk.)
  1. Entertaining. 2. Picnicking. 3. Menus. I. Title. II. Series.
TX731.L55 2005
641.5'78–dc22

                    2005012629

Printed in the United States of America
05 06 07 08 09 — 5 4 3 2 1

Special Thanks To . . .

Belinda Bass, Pamela Clements,
Katie Cleveland, Lindsey Cleveland,
Kate Glass, Jennifer Greenstein,
David Leach, Colleen Nelson,
Barb Rishaw, Paul Shepherd,
Chuck Stephens, Larry Stone

Contents

Welcome to the most comprehensive guide to tailgating ever created. In the following pages you will learn everything you need to know to be the envy of your family, your friends, and—most importantly—everybody else in the parking lot.

There are several components to a successful tailgate party: the tools and setup, the dress and spirit, the food and drinks, the friends and fun. *The Ultimate Tailgater's Handbook* will help you with all of them. Well, almost. You're on your own when it comes to finding friends.

We will also teach you how to prepare for your game- or race-day party. In addition to checklists and planning guides, you'll find a Resources section that will become your friend (well, we did help you find one friend). In the Resources section you'll learn where to locate just about everything you need, including tailgating information for all 32 NFL stadiums, 32 NASCAR tracks, and every school belonging to a conference affiliated with the Bowl Championship Series. That's more than 175 venues in all. This is why we are confident that there's never before been a book like this.

But not everything fits into this book. You'll find additional tailgating tips, games, recipes, and links at www.theultimatetailgater.com.

The Web site is also where we're searching for America's Ultimate Tailgater. Click on the link and you can post a picture of your tailgate party and tell us why we should select you as America's Ultimate Tailgater. Who knows, you might make it onto the Web site, receive an Ultimate Tailgater prize, or even be included in the next edition of *The Ultimate Tailgater's Handbook*.

But, as much fun as you'll have on the Web site and reading this book, the ultimate purpose of all of this knowledge is to help you have more fun at your tailgate. You'll host a better party, wear better clothes, eat better food, and become the ultimate tailgater you've always wanted to be. Just don't get cocky about it. You haven't won our contest yet.

But enough of the preliminaries . . .
let's get ready to tailgate!

History of Tailgating

The first tailgaters really weren't tailgaters at all. At least not in the sense we now think of them. Horses carried these revelers to their destination. Horse tails not being the best place to sit or set up a party, these fans spread out on the ground. It was several years later, spurred by the mass production of the Model T, that Americans began to evolve into the parking-lot fanatics who circle stadiums today.

The car allowed us to go places easily and to take our friends and food with us. Is anything more American than the noble spirit of adventure and the twin loves of healthy competition and the All-U-Can-Eat buffet? The tailgate unites these great joys. In the strictest sense, any automotive eating arrangement might qualify as tailgating. Without the surrounding atmosphere of competition, however, the dining experience falls somewhere in the category of picnicking.

The modern tailgate likely has its roots in college football, first played at College Field in New Brunswick, New Jersey, between Rutgers and Princeton in November 1869. Local authorities insist it was both a fine game and a fine party. The party and its basic elements, though, might have much earlier origins. Two historical events in particular are worth mentioning. Each occurred only a few years before the landmark Rutgers-Princeton game, and together they speak

to both the role of managed conflict in bringing people together socially and the basic American approach to fully mobile, vehicle-based cuisine.

Consider the Battle of Manassas in July 1861. Enthusiastic Union supporters from the Washington, D.C., area arrived with baskets of food and shouts of "Go

Big Blue!" to watch the opening dry land battle in America's Civil War. Historians generally agree this was a case of the right idea at the wrong time, war not being a spectator sport. Still, for those who attended, there was socializing and tradition, tension and excitement. And on that day, there was even precedent set for future upsets by Southeastern Conference teams against their northern opponents. Most importantly, the incident effectively established clear boundaries and regional differences in tailgating traditions. Clearly, the idea appealed to hungry partisan supporters. They simply needed another eight years for a more limited field of battle to be created.

The second historical event evokes a debt of gratitude all tailgaters should acknowledge. It is owed to that renowned and forward-looking American, Charles Goodnight. In 1866 Goodnight, a Texas rancher and entrepreneurial bon vivant, addressed the cowboys' need for a rolling chow hall by transforming a U.S. Army Studebaker wagon into the first chuck wagon. The design was simple, compact, and enduring. In fact, Goodnight's design for a fully equipped mobile kitchen differs very little  from that hauled for a day or a weekend by the modern tailgater. Goodnight's failure to foresee the need for pizza ovens and satellite uplinks in no way diminishes his contribution.

In hindsight, the marriage of football and the chuck wagon clearly seems cosmically ordained. As football spread, so did the tailgate *event,* so that tailgating has become the means by which American fans of sports from football to NASCAR gather to celebrate their teams. The one constant is the love of being with people we know while being surrounded by people we don't, knowing we are all part of the collective enthusiasm for a school, a team, an event, an idea bigger than ourselves.

Tailgating variations are related to regional tastes in food and the quality and particulars of local custom. At Hampden-Sydney College or the University of Mississippi, for example, tailgaters don't show up in less than a coat and tie or semiformal seasonal dress. On the other hand, dressing to the nines for tailgating in the infield at Talladega can establish you as an outsider. Ideally, there are no outsiders at tailgating events, at least not among supporters of the same team or driver. Your tailgate should be an occasion to meet and greet any number of people you might not otherwise acknowledge. After all, if you're going to be friendly with only the people at your tailgate, just invite them over to your house and spare yourself the trouble of setting up in the parking lot. But the ultimate tailgaters already know this.

We are now in an era of very great tailgating, a time of innovation and of elaboration. Getting here required the intersection of fate on the field and design in industry—such as might have occurred at the 1973 Sugar Bowl, when college football fans from around the country congregated in the parking lot of the Superdome. The Notre Dame–Alabama matchup is important for the way it brought together supporters from different socioeconomic, geographic, and even spiritual backgrounds and did so at a time when there was the highest

probability that many people might have arrived in and set up their celebration behind a 1972 Oldsmobile Vista Cruiser, a 1972 Chrysler Town and Country, or even a brand-new 1973 Chevrolet Caprice wagon. These were the heady days of serious wagons with serious tailgates. That particular game-day experience may well have inspired America's present desire for the great tailgating event that continues to grow and call out to the spirited and hungry.

But thirty years later, chances are those 1970s fans sitting on their beefy tailgates wouldn't recognize today's tailgate party.

A lot has changed since Richard Nixon was in the White House. Those serious wagons have been replaced by serious SUVs (some almost big enough to carry that 1973 Caprice wagon) and serious RVs (some of which could hold that Caprice *and* a 1972 Town and Country).

During the late 1980s and the 1990s, tailgating took on a life of its own and became a social movement of sorts. As gas grills became more portable and coolers grew wheels, rows of parking spots became communities—some with their own names and flags. The ultimate tailgates in these lots are almost worthy of being judged along the lines of parade floats.

Did we mention the satellite dishes? There's a good chance that parking-lot hum you hear is a generator powering a TV tuned to one of those satellite football packages.

And TV networks aren't the only marketers who have leveraged this opportunity. Don't believe us? Type "tailgating" into a search engine and see how many results you get (it was 887,000 when we wrote this). These purveyors of tailgating supplies range from mom-and-pops to major retailers, between them generating millions of dollars a year in tailgate-related retail sales.

Many people are willing to spend big for the ultimate day in the parking lot. How much? Hammacher Schlemmer & Co., for instance, sells the Grill-and-Cooler Tailgate Set for $3,000 . . . and that doesn't even include the food. But everyone from Ball Park Franks, to Kraft, to Tabasco, to your neighborhood grocery has tailgating fare to fill the food gap.

The draws that pull today's well-equipped, well-dressed, well-fed fan to the parking lot are the same ones that drew that crowd in 1869: the friends, the party, the game. In fact, two out of three are sufficient for some fans. And probably in that order. One survey found 30 percent of tailgaters never set foot in the stadium.

Tailgating Gear

Just as teams need the right coaches, players, and equipment, tailgaters need the right planners, provisions, and materials. The following is a general list of essential supplies. How elaborately you assemble these items is, of course, entirely up to you, your enthusiasm, and your team and party spirit, not to mention the size of your wallet. The good news is all of these items are available in a range of prices, and each adds to an enjoyable experience. It's possible you might get by without one or two of the particulars listed below; others, however, are so basic that without them your game-day event falls into the lesser category of "parking-lot get-together."

GRILLS

Tailgates offer the ideal environment for less-experienced chefs to develop their culinary skills. Perfection is not important. Everyone is having too good a time to notice if something hasn't been prepared quite right; their primary focus is on the team or the game. An adventurous cook can also exploit this dynamic, seizing the opportunity to push the envelope and try something new. A tailgate chef rarely experiences the pressures dealt with by cooks preparing dinner for the boss or that first date. Use the tailgate to experiment with your cooking interests and bring something new and delightful to your moveable feast. That experiment might best begin over a fire.

The choice of fire is your first decision. Charcoal versus gas. It's an ancient debate—if you consider the 1939 World's Fair in New York ancient. Before then the debate was charcoal versus wood. But no one would lug logs to a tailgate. The debate boils down to flavor (charcoal) versus convenience (gas). While most people certainly would agree that flavorful food is best, you must admit that few things are more convenient than pushing a button to start a flame.

CHARCOAL GRILLS: These are the noble and venerable workhorses of open-air cooking. Think of them as your link to the dim and distant past, as campfires raised to a comfortable cooking height. There are two schools of thought on grills. One contends that when our ancient ancestors first stood upright they quickly devised the grill so that they might never again need to stoop. The other maintains that the grill is one of the few pieces our ancestors took with them when they left paradise. The debate cannot be resolved here.

A charcoal grill has its advantages. It cooks hotter and it's easier to use for smoking foods. Not only that, you've also got to admit that the inner pyro in you loves lighting and playing with fire. But charcoal grills can be messy, they cook somewhat unevenly, and you sometimes have to keep stoking the coals.

Grills are available in many sizes, price ranges, and shapes (if you limit your conception of shape to round and rectangular). The proliferation of team and school gear begs the question of why more tailgaters have not pursued team- and school-specific grill colors. Consider this your chance to start a trend.

When shopping for your ultimate tailgate's charcoal grill, keep an eye out for a few things. First, look for sturdy construction. You'd be well advised to look for one with optional side tables. No one likes to see his or her food prepped on a paper towel that barely covers the asphalt.

If you like to smoke foods, you'll want a front-loading unit or one with a hinged grill gate. This will make life easier for you when adding wood chips to the coals.

No matter what's on your menu, be sure to buy a unit with vents on the top and bottom to adjust airflow (which is what controls your heat) and a tightly fitting dome so you can do indirect grilling.

Of course, the charcoal grill needs fuel if it's going to be any good to you. Don't neglect the charcoal—be sure to buy some that will light easily and burn a long time. When you pack your fuel, think about how long you will need to keep the fire going. Bring *enough* charcoal for the event. Few sights are as tragic as the vegetable kebab or hamburger languishing in its rawness over a single hot coal.

A Note on Ashes: If you cook with charcoal or use wood to smoke foods, you'll need to plan ahead for a way to clean your grill when you are finished. Ashes should never be disposed of where they could start a fire or cause damage to the environment. *Always* bring a container for dead ash and make sure your fire is fully extinguished before closing up shop.

GAS GRILLS: In many respects gas grills *are* more convenient for tailgaters (especially if time is the measure of convenience). Gas grills require very little setup. Cooking temperatures can be achieved in minutes. A simple twist of a knob easily allows you to regulate a heat that will then remain constant. An added benefit is that the propane tank will last much longer than a pile

of coals. The average, full-sized propane tank will burn for up to twenty hours. Barring some sort of catastrophic event, gas grill chefs do not have to worry about extinguishing their fires. They can simply turn their fires off. All this combines to spell E-A-S-E at the tailgate event.

When buying a gas grill for your ultimate tailgate, look for one with at least two heat zones, again for indirect grilling. A built-in gas gauge and thermometer are a big help, as is a drip pan that is easy to empty and clean. Although we'll go into more detail later, it's worth mentioning here that you would be well served to find a grill with a smoker box, side burner, and rotisserie to enhance your game-day menu. And remember: check for sturdy construction and a good warranty.

GRILL TOOLS AND ACCESSORIES

Of course, you don't want to cook your tailgate feast with just your hands. You're going to need tools, and having the right grill tools is essential. Many of these are obvious items to bring along; others aren't, but all will improve your tailgate cooking experience.

TONGS: These are handy because they are good for everything from prodding and flipping foods to fishing obstinate grill-ables out of the coals to choosing the perfect corndog.

SPATULAS: Keep a variety on hand. For starters, have one that's rigid and another that's more flexible. Short and long styles provide added flexibility.

GRILL BRUSHES: Keep those grills clean and your food free of last weekend's charred remains. Some brushes have at least two kinds of bristles, giving you more options for removing different types of cooked-on food.

KNIVES: Even if you've done your prep work before the tailgate, you never know when you'll need a good knife. Make sure it's sharp and is set aside for only the cook's use. This will keep the cook and the bartender from having to trade or share tools. The ultimate tailgater will have one chef's knife and one serrated knife to be ready for any dish.

APRONS: A good apron is one that serves several purposes and works as basic safety gear to wear around a grill. It can protect clothes from stains and burns, hold items such as that snazzy meat thermometer you got for Christmas, and give you a place to wipe your hands. Aprons emblazoned with your favorite team's name and logo are widely available.

TOWELS: Cooks need to keep these within arm's reach for wiping hands and mopping up spills of marinade. Keep two or three around your tailgating space.

INSTANT-READ MEAT THERMOMETERS: Quite simply, these handy gadgets could save your life one day. Believe it. Some meat thermometers double as meat forks. That gives you two tools in one. Others are small and clip like pens onto your apron pocket. If the lifesaving function of the meat thermometer isn't enough to inspire you to have one, then consider the unquestionably professional look they offer the cook. Chefs who feel confident will cook that way, and that almost always translates to better food.

HATS: Strictly speaking, the hat is not an *essential* piece of equipment. That said, some sort of hat identifying the chef is always appropriate. Moreover, the chef's hat is easily decorated to demonstrate team allegiance and can be one more item to help tie together the tailgate's general theme. For example, at your fiesta tailgate (see pages 55–57) you might enhance a traditional chef's hat with a wide sombrero brim.

With your tools in place, it's time to enhance your tailgating experience with grill accessories. No, you do not *have to* have any of these, but the ultimate tailgater will give serious consideration to them.

SIDE BURNERS: Propane-powered side burners are, as you might have guessed, specific to the gas grill. A side burner is surely the single most useful addition to the basic gas grill unit, giving the gas grill a level of versatility not available with its charcoal cousin. Side burners function exactly like a stovetop. They can either stand alone or, in many cases, be attached to the main grill.

The other most-common accessories for grills are not specific to charcoal or gas models, and any grilling enthusiast may want to consider adding these:

WARMING RACKS: Most gas grills come with built-in warming racks, but if your grill does not have them, consider these for your first grill addition. Warming racks allow you to keep cooked food hot without reducing it to cinders.

STEAMERS: These do exactly what their name implies. What might not be so obvious is the wide range of tailgate food items that readily lend themselves to steaming. Steamed foods can include everything from vegetables to fresh dumplings to shellfish, broadening the horizons of your tailgate's menu.

DUTCH OVENS AND OTHER POTS, PANS, AND SKILLETS: These

utensils further increase the capabilities of your grill. Stews and sauces, soups and chilies, fried and sautéed foods now become tailgating possibilities. Few people cook at home without pots and pans; why cook in the parking lot without them? Never overlook the tangible and spiritual benefits to your tailgate of the shrimp, crawfish, crab, or lobster boil.

SKEWERS AND KEBAB RACKS:

It is almost impossible to conceive of a grilling occasion when the kebab is unwelcome. Be prepared, though. Any kebab aficionado knows that just plopping the kebab onto the grill can cause problems. Good skewers and a rack to lift the food off the grill are helpful for producing high-quality kebabs. Skewers are made of metal or wood (the metal ones usually have a ring on one end) and need to be able to securely hold their ingredients in place. The best skewers for that are flat or square ones; food tends to slip and slide more on round ones. Some racks are designed to permit easy rotation of the skewer over the heat. Many chefs consider them essential gear.

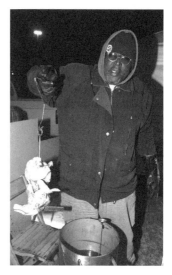

ROTISSERIES:

This grill accessory may well separate the dilettante from the devotee. Apart from providing an additional burner, the rotisserie is the one accessory that most fundamentally alters what your grill can do for you. Nearly all major grill manufacturers offer rotisseries for both charcoal and gas grills. Think about it—you can put just about anything on a spit. Be bold! But keep in mind that in *most* cases—say about 95 percent of the time—grill rotisseries require a power source (see **portable generators** on page 22).

DEEP FRYERS:

If you have a power source handy, a deep fryer is a fabulous addition to your tailgate setup. Modern deep fryers designed for home use are remarkably inexpensive and easy to use. Many home models are self-contained, so there is no danger of oil spatters and no need to empty the oil reservoir when you're finished frying. These machines are quite safe when used properly. Can there really be any good reason not to offer the joys of fries, onion rings, or a fried turkey at your tailgate?

PORTABLE GENERATORS: Although there are no litmus tests to determine the levels of tailgater enthusiasm, there is clearly a dividing line between tailgates with and without their own portable generators. A lot can be accomplished on battery power alone, but a portable generator will help you do more; for instance, it can power that rotisserie on your grill.

Portable generators have come a long way. New designs make them attractive options for the ultimate tailgater. Almost silent, or at least very quiet, models are available. Generally speaking, even a relatively small generator can meet the average tailgater's needs to power up a music system, party lighting, TV set, and blender. More elaborate setups require more power, obviously. Big changes in generator requirements occur when you move beyond small stereos and kitchen appliances to bigger and more powerful items like refrigerators, microwave ovens, and multiple TV sets with satellite dishes. So when pondering how to power up your tailgate, consider the type of unit you want (or wish to lug around in your vehicle), the wattage you'll need, and the features that suit you.

The most important feature you want in your new generator is an electric starter. Ditch the idea of getting one with a pull cord. Yanking one over and over might allow you to relive your days as a youth mowing yards, but the charm rubs off quickly. Don't forget a wheel kit, either; your back will thank us for that tip. Also on the list is runtime . . . the size of the tank. That's what determines the amount of time the generator will run before your lights, TV, and tailgate go dark.

If you want to compare generators for your tailgate use, you'll find a Generator Feature Checklist at www.theultimatetailgater.com.

THE BAR

The bar can be as simple as a cooler filled with ice and soft drinks. Or it can be much more involved. Plenty of deeply invested tailgaters bring fully functioning bars to their events. Not everyone can do this, but everyone can make decisions about the limits of what they will serve and then make the necessary preparations. Some basic questions to ask: soft drinks?—you may not even need cups. Mixed drinks?—you'll need cups and a whole lot more.

The portable bar can become a measure of one's civility. Its completeness and complexity demonstrate the depth of your hospitality and desire to cater to your guests' happiness. Perhaps all you need to supply are a bottle opener and a corkscrew, and your friends will bring the rest. In other cases, you may want to anticipate the particular tastes of, say, your discerning aunt. Maybe she relishes a crisp homemade lemonade in the morning but prefers an obscure single malt scotch in the afternoon (or at least anytime after five o'clock Greenwich Mean Time). As the tailgate host, your ability to know and provide for your guests can be a source of tremendous satisfaction to everyone.

DRINK ACCESSORIES: If you plan to serve drinks, make sure you pack a bottle opener and a corkscrew (often a combined tool) and a jigger for measuring. You might also want to bring along a guide to mixing drinks. If mixed drinks are served, you will need a shaker and a strainer. You should also have a knife and cutting board reserved for the bartender's use. This prevents the cook from having to share

equipment. Napkins and swizzle sticks are always nice to have on hand. Both add color and a festive touch to the occasion and can serve to tie in the theme of your event. At your luau tailgate, for example, swizzle sticks should clearly take the form of tiny and gaily colored umbrellas.

BAR CADDIES: Bartenders around the world swear by their bar caddies. These compartmentalized covered trays are inexpensive and allow you to store and present a wide assortment of garnishes. Having a caddie makes it easy to do your prep work ahead of time and store your condiments safely. Quite frankly, the professional look you gain by having one is a clear and indisputable bonus.

BLENDERS AND ICE CRUSHERS: If you have electricity, a blender is a wonderful addition to your bar. If all you need to do is crush ice, the hand-cranked ice crusher fits the bill. Although it won't blend drinks, it will crush ice as well as any of its motorized counterparts.

ICE: One basic rule is that you can never have too much ice. With the exception of those quasi-professional tailgaters who can make their own ice on-site, once you run out, you can almost never get more—without real inconvenience. Remember, the first question to ask about ice is not "How do I store it?" (see the next entry on **coolers**) but rather, "What do I need ice for?" The answer will almost always be "for my food and my drinks," but this deceptively simple answer masks one of the most complex decisions the tailgater faces. Be precise in your calculations: what will you need to keep cold, and for how long? Use separate coolers for food and drinks. Using separate coolers will help keep your ice for drinks generally clean—and you can always keep it bagged, too. It will also help keep the drink ice free from serious contamination from the chicken and beef you didn't seal properly and that leaked juices. If having two coolers means you need to buy another one, so be it. It's a worthwhile investment. There are two surefire ways to have a lousy tailgate, and contaminating your food inside your ice chests is one of them. The other one is letting your food go bad in the sun. We'll get to that in a moment.

COOLERS: As for the coolers (aka ice chests), there are many fine models available. Even the $1.99 Styrofoam cooler is better than none at all. Get as big a cooler as you can easily transport. They are like closets or attics or basements—if you have the room, you'll find something to put in it. In selecting a cooler, look for substantial hinges, a good tight seal around the lid, and a secure lock. Check on the availability of accessories such as interior dividers and tray inserts. These can prove phenomenally helpful. Make sure you get a cooler with a drain on it. Perhaps the greatest recent innovation in coolers is the addition of wheels on some models. Why in the world would you carry your loaded ice chest when you can roll it? And second only to the wheel for improving the usefulness of the cooler is the split lid that allows you to keep one section of your cooler sealed while you fish out what you need from another.

There are certain items you should gather, put somewhere safe, and load up every time you head to the stadium. You will need them week in and week out. Without them your tailgate will suffer from embarrassment and error. We call these items "the basics."

TABLES:
A corollary to the rule for ice is you probably can't have enough flat space to work on, to eat from, or to set your drinks down on. Tables need to be sturdy and portable. Make sure they have a locking mechanism on the legs. If they don't, you will want to review carefully the entries on **first-aid kits** (pages 28–29) and **towels** (page 27). Your table is essentially the focal point of your tailgate. Don't neglect it—cover it in tablecloths in team colors and decorate it with centerpieces that announce your tailgate theme and team loyalty.

Try to arrange table space for each separate area of your tailgate. This helps avoid clutter and crowding. Provide some sort of area to function as your buffet or assembly area for food. If you have a bar, make a space for it. Above all, *don't crowd the cook*, who needs his or her own separate prep station apart from the main spread. The cooler lid is not a table or efficient workspace. Nothing upsets the tailgate applecart quite like having to repeatedly move everything off the cooler to reach what's inside. It's a no-win situation for the person using the lid as a tabletop as well as a time-delay nuisance for the person thirsting for a drink. All of this can easily be avoided by bringing enough flat space to work on.

CUTTING BOARDS: This is a subset of the table. Make sure you have one. Better still: have more than one. The cook will surely need one and should not have to borrow one from the bar. The bartender will need one, too. No one wants a lime wedge that has been sliced on the asphalt, and ever since Uncle Lucius lost that finger, no one is willing to try slicing the limes in his or her hands.

CHAIRS: In bygone days the great tailgates themselves were large enough to seat fifteen comfortably, but few vehicles now offer such accommodations. Traditionally, the tailgate is not a sit-down affair. But again, you know your own needs and limitations, and those of your guests. You'll find a tremendous number of portable chairs on the market, ranging from the most basic three-legged folding campstools to collapsible recliners with built-in insulated cup holders. If you're only going to tailgate and not go into the event, you're almost surely going to want to sit down. Some balance between comfort and portability is your goal.

TENTS, TARPS, AND TOWELS: There's more to the tailgate than keeping the drinks cold and serving the food hot. You also need to be prepared to keep your guests, yourself, and, yes, your food out of the sun. If you are an ultimate tailgater, you might already have a tent that you set up at your events. Tents help distinguish the occasional game-day tailgater from the more regular, fanatical sort. A tent is an investment, but one that lasts a long time and is useful in 1,001 ways. Before balking at the price, remember that a tent will pay for itself the first time you're under it in a surprise thunderstorm. Tents also bring a consistency to your tailgate. They are landmarks. Fellow tailgaters trying to find their way back after the game in a crowded parking lot have an easier time if they can spot your tent. Tents also offer a structure from which to hang your lighting, banners, flags, and opponents' effigies. Tarpaulins are handy to have around, too. They can serve as ground covers in muddy conditions, be strung up as awnings to block rain or sun, or be used as tablecloths (in a pinch). Similarly, towels are a commonsense item. They're good for everything from soaking up spills to drying off after sudden (or steady) rainstorms. One very useful thing to do with a towel is insulate your cooler—especially if you have no tent or tarp to keep it in the shade.

TRASH CANS: Bringing your own may seem like overkill, but think again. A full-size model can hold a bunch of tailgate gear in transit. Even a small model, like the tall kitchen size, can hold more stuff than you might think. Unpacked and lined with a bag, the trash can helps everyone keep your area orderly. The only drawback to having your own trash can is that other, less-organized tailgaters may want to use yours. Consider this a great opportunity to set a good example by showing the shortsighted how to dispose of the remains of their day.

FIRST-AID KITS: This might not be the first thing you think of while packing for your tailgate. However, you can bet it will be first thing you look for when your buddy overturns the deep fryer on someone's foot or Uncle Lucius swears he can still cut a lime wedge with only nine fingers. You never expect an accident, but you can be ready for the unforeseen by taking the time to assemble some basic first-aid products.

While the cell phone may be the first piece of first-aid equipment you reach for in an emergency, don't neglect to assemble a complete first-aid kit. Even in a serious emergency, you'll need to do something to help the injured between the time you call for help and the time the help arrives.

Not all situations requiring first-aid treatment are serious emergencies. Prepare for any first-aid contingency by creating a clearly labeled and immediately identifiable box and then packing it with the following basic items, as well as anything else you think you might need:

> Alcohol swabs/antiseptic wipes
>
> Triple antibiotic ointment—useful for any abrasion or cut
>
> Hydrocortisone cream—for insect stings and bites, also helpful for rashes from allergic reactions
>
> Adhesive bandages
>
> Sterile gauze pads
>
> First-aid tape
>
> Scissors
>
> One or two elastic bandages—good for wrapping sprained ankles
>
> Burn creams—including sunburn creams
>
> Ibuprofen or acetaminophen
>
> Aspirin
>
> Antacids
>
> Tweezers
>
> Disposable instant cold pack
>
> Thermometer
>
> Plastic/latex gloves—at least two pairs
>
> Blanket (not necessarily in the first-aid box, but have one nearby)
>
> Cobra antivenin—well, you know your terrain best

PRIVATE BATHROOMS: Don't laugh. Increasingly, tailgaters are bringing their own porta-potties to events—and not just the tailgaters with RVs. The convenience of your own restroom is appealing, but actually having one at the tailgate is a huge step for most people to take. If you take it, take it seriously. There's really nothing pleasant about raw sewage, and without a professional system for containing what you and your guests could not, you may want to stick to nearby public facilities—you know, the kind hooked up to municipal plumbing. Otherwise, set up as close as you can to the folks with the big RV and make friends.

Dressing the Part

While tailgating is about the food, the drink, and the friends, it's also a party. And we all know we have to dress for a party.

But the tailgate party is different. For one, you're outside. It rains there. And snows. So you need to be prepared for that, since the chances of the sun shining on your party week after week are slim. Very slim.

It also gets hot. Or cold. So you need to dress for that, too. Keep in mind that dressing the part is not just about fashion; it's about safety, too. Nothing kills the party like an ambulance coming to pick up your friend who has collapsed from heatstroke. More about dressing for the weather a little later.

First, let's talk ultimate tailgating fashion.

Fashion is revealing. What you wear makes a statement about you. It places you in a group. It can be fun. Tailgating fashion is no different. It just involves more logos and face paint.

It is important to wear your team colors. Don't worry, you won't be alone. Licensed sports product sales top $12 billion a year. That'll buy a lot of cheese heads and jerseys. But you don't have to wear a player's uniform number on your chest to fit in. In fact, at some tailgates where formal attire is more common, that might get you kicked out.

There are many definitions of dressing the part for a tailgate. Some of the nuances are geographic. Some are socioeconomic. Some are defined by the sport. Some are defined by . . . well, we don't know what makes people want to strip down in thirty-degree weather and paint a letter on their chest. But we're glad they do; they make for great conversation.

The first thing you must do when gazing at your closet on game day is determine what type of tailgater you are. Are you a casual or a loyal fan? Is formal attire more appropriate for your crowd? Are you an extreme fan who will stop at nothing to show your support? Or does your sport have its own culture? Tough questions, we know. But that's why we're here. On the next few pages you'll meet some of these fans. Look them over closely and see if you see yourself in any of them. Chances are you will. Then you'll know exactly which hanger to pull off the rack.

Casual Tailgater Attire
for Men

ENTHUSIASTIC GRIN
Open mouth is a time-saving device for cheering, eating, and drinking.

BASEBALL CAP
Not necessarily team specific, and certainly not new. At college football games the hat should be cotton with a logo—either academic or corporate. At some NASCAR events hats may be polyester with slogans about fishing, hunting, or racing.

PAINTED CHEST
Acceptable with either school colors or with a letter forming part of the school or team name. In cold weather this look goes a long way toward showing your devotion to your team and getting seen on TV.

FOOTBALL
Handy for tossing about to waste time before the game. Also helps to make you unmistakable as a fan.

UNMARKED PLASTIC TUMBLER
Probably should not exceed 64 ounces.

BELTS
Optional, but always in good taste.

SHORTS
An excellent choice in warm weather, but if shorts are all you are wearing make them nice shorts.

BOTTLE OPENER
Someone, possibly you, will need one and appreciate your forethought.

The casual male tailgater is usually young, often still in college. He would have a hard time deciding which part of the game-day experience is more important to him—the tailgate or the actual game. He is frequently found in various stages of undress regardless of the outside temperature. His enthusiasm, however, is never dampened by rain, sleet, or snow, nor is it wilted by too much sun. If you'll just pour him another cold drink, he'll be happy to sing you the fight song one more time.

BOOT
Provides insulation against cold and spills.

Casual Tailgater Attire
for Women

HEADBAND
In team colors. Effective for ear warming without damaging hairstyle.

POM-POM
Excellent for spirited cheering; useful for self-defense or as a swizzle stick.

SCHOOL MASCOT OR INITIAL FACE PAINT
A socially acceptable, gender-specific alternative to painting large letters on bare chests.

UNMARKED PLASTIC TUMBLER
Probably should not exceed 32 ounces.

DOWN-FILLED JACKET
Warm enough to keep you comfortable and soft enough to encourage sharing warmth with others.

LONG PANTS
An obvious choice in colder weather.

SKIRT
In warmer weather provides a glimpse of the remains of a summer tan and offers a sense of casual elegance—especially useful if your date has abandoned all refinement in favor of chest painting.

COMFORTABLE SHOE
Know your tailgate terrain. Heels may be fine, but not in soggy ground or mud.

As with the casual male, the casual female tailgater is usually college age. For her, the game being played on the field is secondary to the games being played before kickoff. The social aspects of tailgating are what interest her most and the reason she never misses a game. Tailgating is an opportunity to see and be seen; to eat, drink, and catch up with friends; to show off her team spirit and her cute little outfit.

Loyal Fan Tailgater Attire
for Men

GOOD FOOD
Large quantities are always essential to a successful tailgate.

BEVERAGE
An insulated foam holder keeps drinks cold. It also prevents fingers from freezing to the can in cold weather.

BINOCULARS
Handy in the stadium to get a better look at the field, but also useful pregame for spying on other tailgaters or finding lost friends who have wandered off.

TEAM APRON
An excellent way to show your enthusiasm. Obviously, this is a more useful accessory for the cook than for others.

SMALL TV
Allows the cook to keep abreast of the pregame show even over in his work space. May be electric or battery powered.

This is the man who lives for the tailgate (not to be confused with the man who lives for the team; see Extreme Fan, page 41). Yes, he loves his team, but he also loves the opportunity to get together with his family and friends and grill up some burgers and steaks, rehash the season so far, and make predictions for the games to come.

Loyal Fan Tailgater Attire
for Women

HAIR ACCESSORIES
Here again is a place to show team support. Scrunchies, ribbons, headbands, and—for the fashion forward—hair extensions all come in a variety of colors and will certainly be available in a combination appropriate for your team.

EARRINGS
Ideally these will be showy and display your team's colors or logo.

WINEGLASS OR TUMBLER
Hand–painted by you or your friends in team colors or with the team insignia.

BRACELETS
Another place to show your spirit. Charm bracelets with team charms are an excellent option. A more simple option is simply to purchase plastic bangles in team colors.

NICE JEANS
Jeans (or heavier pants when the weather turns cooler) are clean and tidy and worn with comfortable, sensible shoes. This allows for freedom of movement—most likely to be in the form of jumping up and down in support of your team.

This woman is here for her team. It's great to be with her friends and family, too, but her main purpose at the tailgate is to support her boys. She will dress comfortably and casually, and accessorize with as many items as possible to display her team loyalty.

Formal Tailgater Attire
for Men

NECKTIE
Your choice in tie offers a chance to show team allegiance. Bowties are an excellent alternative since they are harder to spill upon.

BLUE BLAZER
It's always appropriate.

SHIRT
Should be clean and pressed.

MARTINI
Do not skimp on stemware. Nothing ruins a good drink faster than plastic stemware.

WOOL BLAZER AND VEST
Provide you with layers of warmth while still looking classy.

The formal male tailgater is most often found at college games in the South or Northeast. He is of the belief that any social occasion, whether indoors or outdoors, requires proper dress, proper cocktails, and proper decorum. While all of the items shown here are essential, leeway is given to the men based upon their age. Undergraduates are frequently more rumpled and bleary-eyed at morning tailgates than the school's older alumni.

KHAKIS
Like the shirt, these should be clean and pressed.

NICE SHOES
Do not ruin a perfectly nice outfit with a poor footwear choice. Saddle oxfords, loafers, or boots are all fine choices.

SUMMER | **WINTER**

Formal Tailgater Attire
for Women

EARMUFFS
Keep ears warm without messing up your hair.

JEWELRY
Should be minimal and tasteful. A school ring, a simple bracelet, and earrings really are all that is required.

VEST
A quilted down vest, or whatever is in style this winter, to keep warm.

DRESS
An attractive sundress that is neat and pressed. Tasteful, but not overly trendy.

TOTE
The summer straw tote is a useful place to display team spirit without messing up your outfit. It is also a handy spot to stash water, sunscreen, and those cute little airplane liquor bottles that are ideal for dressing up a soft drink.

Like her male counterpart, the formal female tailgater is most often found at college games in the South or Northeast. However, unlike for the men, there is no degree of leeway allowed for untidiness based on age. Hair should be done, make-up applied, dress carefully chosen for flattering fit and function (that being the ability to last several hours in possibly inclement weather while continuing to fit and flatter).

DUCK BOOT
A sturdy boot or shoe to keep toes warm and offer protection from stomped toes.

Tailgater Attire for **NASCAR**

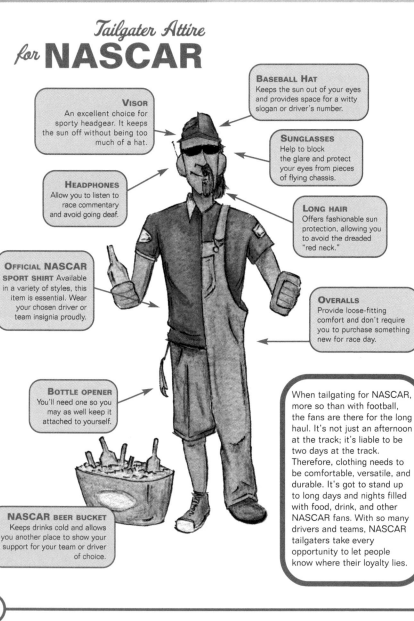

BASEBALL HAT
Keeps the sun out of your eyes and provides space for a witty slogan or driver's number.

VISOR
An excellent choice for sporty headgear. It keeps the sun off without being too much of a hat.

SUNGLASSES
Help to block the glare and protect your eyes from pieces of flying chassis.

HEADPHONES
Allow you to listen to race commentary and avoid going deaf.

LONG HAIR
Offers fashionable sun protection, allowing you to avoid the dreaded "red neck."

OFFICIAL NASCAR SPORT SHIRT Available in a variety of styles, this item is essential. Wear your chosen driver or team insignia proudly.

OVERALLS
Provide loose-fitting comfort and don't require you to purchase something new for race day.

BOTTLE OPENER
You'll need one so you may as well keep it attached to yourself.

NASCAR BEER BUCKET
Keeps drinks cold and allows you another place to show your support for your team or driver of choice.

When tailgating for NASCAR, more so than with football, the fans are there for the long haul. It's not just an afternoon at the track; it's liable to be two days at the track. Therefore, clothing needs to be comfortable, versatile, and durable. It's got to stand up to long days and nights filled with food, drink, and other NASCAR fans. With so many drivers and teams, NASCAR tailgaters take every opportunity to let people know where their loyalty lies.

Tailgater Attire for **Extreme Fans**

HEADGEAR
Headgear is essential. The fire bolt motif here is optional.

DEEP-FRIED TURKEY LEG
Offers pregame sustenance and looks impressive when brandished about. The bone can be saved for angry gesturing at the referees during the game.

ARMOR PLATING
Provides no real function except to look scary and get people out of your way as you work your way through a crowd.

AIR HORN
Color commentary in an aerosol can. It can also be used on boats or to break up dogfights.

SHOES
Exciting foot gear is required, such as this superhero-inspired look.

No definitive explanation can be provided for the costumes worn by extreme fans. These are the fans for whom the tailgate is merely the opening act; the game is their main event. Almost always male (go figure), these fans follow their own artistic muse. The specifics of each outfit spring from their hearts and minds. Typically these costumes radiate an aura of derangement or menace, but some costumes offer a humorous tribute to the fan's team of choice. Every team has a few of these fans and you can most often find them pregame posing for photos with tailgaters less extravagantly dressed.

DRESSING FOR THE WEATHER

Now that you know your tailgate style and what you're wearing, let's talk about whether it's right for the weather. Word plays aside, it is a serious issue and one you must consider before heading to the stadium.

Both football and racing seasons stretch from summer to winter. That means from hot to cold. And in many areas of the country that means from very hot (after all, the Arizona Cardinals play in a desert) to very cold (think the Green Bay Packers in December).

Since the football season kicks off in August, let's talk about dressing for hot weather first.

You may think this is a no-brainer—shorts and a T-shirt. But that's not enough, especially at a tailgate where you're outside for hours and most likely enjoying an alcoholic beverage or two.

A quick science lesson: people suffer heat-related illnesses when the body's temperature-control system gets overloaded. Normally, your body will cool itself by sweating. Sometimes sweating isn't enough. When the humidity is high, sweat doesn't evaporate as quickly, which in turn prevents the body from releasing heat. Factors such as advanced age, obesity, sunburn, and alcohol only exacerbate the problem. The result can be heatstroke or other ailments that can damage the brain and other organs.

The following are some simple rules that will help you stay cool.

1. Drink a lot of fluids. In fact, drink more than your thirst tells you to. And we're talking water here. Beer and alcohol just make matters worse. They do *not* hydrate the body. Dehydration is a serious problem easily prevented. In desert areas, it is especially important to remember to keep drinking fluids since you won't sweat like you usually do (part of that whole "it's a dry heat" thing) so you may not know you're running low.

2. Wear lightweight, light-colored, loose-fitting clothing.

3. Wear a wide-brimmed hat to provide shade and keep your head cool.

4. Wear sunscreen. You should be doing this anyway, but it's especially important in very hot conditions. Be sure to use at least SPF 15 and apply it thirty minutes before you walk out of the house. Read the directions on the sunscreen to know how often to reapply it. One coat might not cut it.

5. Avoid eating heavy meals. They add heat to your body. Instead, eat light foods and eat smaller portions more often. The ultimate tailgater will watch the weather forecast and plan the menu accordingly.

6. Stay in the shade as much as possible. A tent over your tailgate is a great help. If you don't have a tent, use an umbrella or spend some time in the car with the air on, but only if it doesn't create exhaust problems for other tailgaters.

If anyone at your tailgate party exhibits signs of heavy sweating, paleness, weakness, vomiting, dizziness, or fainting, get him or her to a cool area immediately, provide cool (not cold) water, and call for medical help.

Then there's the other extreme. Not dressing appropriately for winter tailgates and games can bring on other symptoms just as serious as heat-related problems. Hypothermia is a serious winter problem, especially among older people whose skin is less sensitive to the cold. That's why, in some cases, they don't experience the signs of exposure to dangerously cold temperatures until it's too late. If anyone at your tailgate experiences violent shivering, stops shivering, has slow breathing with a slow pulse, or seems confused, take him or her to a warm place and call for medical help.

Your cold weather science lesson is about insulation, which prevents the aforementioned problems. Dressing in layers creates room for air pockets that lock in heat. This retains body heat and, if done correctly, will keep you dry. A hat is critical to locking in your body heat, too. Don't think you need one? Worried about your hair? Up to 90 percent of your body heat can be lost through the top of your head. Wear the hat and bring a brush.

Now, dressing in layers doesn't just mean anything on top of anything else. It's important to layer properly.

INNER LAYER: This layer should be a material that "wicks" moisture from your body to help keep you dry and comfortable. (Fashion terms 101: "Wicking" refers to the ability of a fabric to move sweat away from the skin to the surface of the garment. Once there, it evaporates and you stay dry and comfortable. These garments are widely available and usually say on the label that they are made of a wicking material.)

MIDDLE LAYER: The middle layer should trap warm air and hold it in those air pockets we talked about. Depending on how cold it is outside, you may need several middle layers.

OUTER LAYER: This layer needs to provide protection from wind, rain, snow, and other cold-weather beasts. It is important for the outer layer to be water-resistant enough to keep the inner and middle layers dry.

Down and wool are good materials for the middle layers. A number of synthetic materials are also designed especially for this purpose. And just because you're trying to stay warm doesn't mean all these layers need to be thick. Your clothes still need to give you freedom of movement. Remember, it's the science of the air pockets that's keeping you warm.

Lastly, don't forget your feet. If your feet are cold—and you will feel it most in your toes—your whole body is going to feel cold. Wear insulated socks with heavy shoes or boots. Walk around some, too, to help fend off frozen toes.

I t's important to understand one basic thing: you don't just pull into a parking space, toss out a table and some chairs, and pop open a drink. That's not tailgating. That's killing time.

Think of the layout of your tailgate in the sense that you think of the layout of your kitchen. You don't toss the stove next to the breakfast table. The chairs don't go next to the trash. The layout of your parking space is as important to the tailgating experience as the decorations, the food, and how you're dressed.

The important thing here is flow. Just like at a party at your home, you want your tailgate party to flow . . . from the bar, to the conversation area, to the food and around again, while keeping the mess of the kitchen (or in this case, the grill) out of the way.

Some people choose to bring a whole kitchen to their tailgates. Others go for a much more basic setup. You should pick whichever best suits your needs. Remember, though, even the smallest tailgate setup for should be well thought out. If you're more adventurous by nature, you will want to be sure to think through what goes where. You don't want the lava flow from your volcano at your luau tailgate mixing with your salsa. But if the lava flow *is* your salsa . . . now that's an ultimate tailgate setup.

Take a look at the illustrations in this chapter and use them as a guide for your tailgate. Your layout doesn't have to match exactly, but the philosophy of why things are where they are should apply. And let us know how that lava flow–salsa setup turns out.

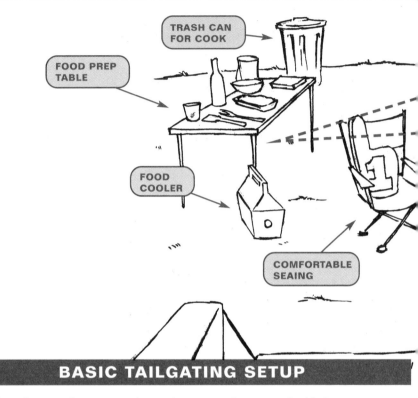

TRASH CAN FOR COOK

FOOD PREP TABLE

FOOD COOLER

COMFORTABLE SEAING

BASIC TAILGATING SETUP

When all you really want is a place to hang out and eat some food before you head into the stadium, your tailgating needs are pretty simple. However, even the simplest of setups requires a little forethought.

Notice the dotted line in the drawing showing the triangular flow that makes this a successful setup. As you can see, the food prep table is a separate station from the buffet table. Give the cook some space. A crowded cook is an angry cook and no one wants that. The grill is set slightly away from the eating and socializing area so you don't engulf your guests in soot. It's also safer to have it away from other flammable items—fire is bad.

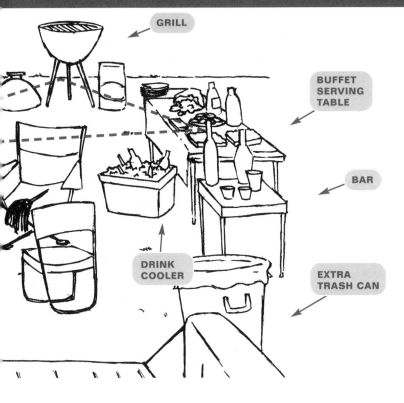

GRILL

BUFFET SERVING TABLE

BAR

DRINK COOLER

EXTRA TRASH CAN

Along with not crowding the cook, it's a good idea not to crowd the bar. Give it its own table. This will allow for easier traffic flow back and forth between the food table and the bar, since you and your guests will not all be trying to pile up at the same four-foot-square card table.

Another couple of items to note: even with a small setup, it's nice to have two trash cans so that the prep area has one and the dining area has one. And you'll see there are two coolers. One for the food prep and one for the bar. If you don't remember why this is a good idea, refer to the entry on **ice** on page 24.

FOOD COOLER

TV

INTERMEDIATE TAILGATING SETUP

You've added more people. You've added more food. And, perhaps the biggest change of all, you've added a power source. Even with the introduction of a small portable generator, certain rules of flow still apply for this intermediate tailgating setup and some additional principles should be considered.

We've still got the triangular flow setup because the cook still needs space. And with more people moving around, it's even more important that the grills be set up out of the way of the immediate traffic flow and that there should be a prep table for the cook. It should be easy for the cook to move from prepping the food, to

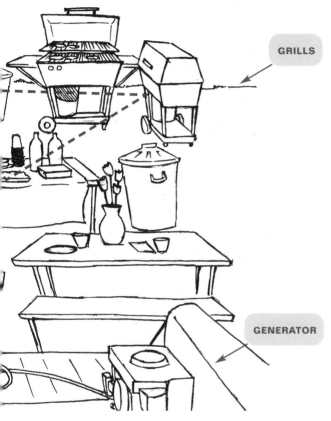

GRILLS

GENERATOR

grilling the food, to serving the food. The triangle is still here, just placed a little differently. If you've added more table space, make sure to make it look nice. Whether you decorate it with flowers or team paraphernalia is up to you.

Now that you have a generator, make sure it is safely out of the way of your guests—at the very least this keeps you from having to shout over it the entire time. Also, make sure to keep power cords out of the way. That old joke about "enjoying your trip" really is only funny the first time someone falls down.

SATELLITE DISH

INFLATABLE MASCOT

GROUND SHAKING SOUND SYSTEM

DEEP FRYER

BIG TV

SERIOUS TAILGATING SETUP

You have graduated from just grilling in a parking lot. This is an event. You've got lots of food, lots of drink, a sound system, lights—you've got it all. Heck, you might even get a news crew to swing by and put your tailgate on TV. But this additional display means additional planning. With this much going on in one parking space, you can't just show up, shove everything out of your car, and hope it works.

Even with the extravagance, you want to begin with the basics. You still need the workspace triangle for the cook. Ideally you'll position this so that the grills don't smoke up the tent. Make sure they have adequate airflow. You'll want to make sure your bar and your buffet table don't crowd each other and that everyone can move around and seat themselves comfortably to see the TV or observe whatever other entertainment you might have arranged. You may also be wise to scatter extra trash cans around since you'll have a larger crowd and more trash.

With the basics out of the way, you can now focus on the features that will turn this into an ultimate tailgate. Be creative and don't be afraid to build props, design cutouts, use inflatable characters, and so on. Have you ever watched the show *Monster House* on television? That's what we're talking about.

All of this means there will be several power cables, cords, and guide wires around in this setup. Make sure to keep them out from underfoot—particularly the one for the deep fryer. You really don't want someone accidentally turning over a vat of hot oil. Come up with ways to keep the cords out of the way and tidy. If you really have a lot of cords, consider getting some stakes for them or buying cable covers like the ones for your home audio/video system. These covers can get expensive if you're running them the length of your tailgate, so use them for the high traffic areas and everywhere else use tape markers to warn your guests.

Themes for Your Tailgate

Variety is the spice of life. There's no reason it cannot also be the spice of tailgating. If you find yourself tiring of the standard fare of burgers, ribs, and coleslaw, you might consider mixing things up a bit by embracing a theme for your next tailgate. Choose a theme based on a season, a type of food, a national holiday, or any of your special interests. Some groups of tailgaters take turns during the season picking a theme for their parties. This is a great way to learn about new foods and new drinks. And even new entertainment: the attention attracted by your troupe of can-can dancers brought in for your French-themed tailgate will allow you to meet new people (certainly, they will draw a crowd). Five options for themed tailgates are outlined in the following pages. Remember, the level of extravagance in your tailgate is entirely up to you, and these are merely ideas to get your creative juices flowing. Once they are swirling freely around your brain, take a look under the heading of Decorations in the Resources section of this handbook. You will find a listing of several Web sites and sources, whose wares will help you add dimension and depth to your chosen theme. Who knows? While browsing the Internet looking for grass skirts and tiki god statues, you might just come across an item that inspires you in a whole new direction.

FIESTA TAILGATE

Unlike holiday-inspired or season-driven tailgates, any time is the right time for a fiesta. The farther your tailgate is from the Mexican border, the greater your opportunity to capitalize on the fiesta theme. Consider the exotic appeal your fiesta tailgate will have at the next Minnesota Vikings game. Wherever you are, throw yourself into the event. The "fiesta" is a broad platform on which to build. Salsa and chips and a lime wedge in your *cerveza* are a beginning, but they aren't an end unto themselves.

The recent explosion of interest in southwestern cooking makes setting up your menu much easier. Build on the basics and explore new ways of preparing your *pollo* and *carne*. Opportunities abound for creating exciting décor that will reinforce the direction you take in exploring Mexican culture. If you are moving toward tacos and fajitas, then you will almost certainly want to get some team-colored sombreros and ponchos. Serapes are usually inexpensive, make fine table coverings, and can add a tremendous amount of color to your setup.

Think along the lines of creating a scene. Stringing up chili pepper lights is a great way to begin, but also consider cutting out large cardboard saguaro cacti to frame your tailgate or support your tent. The ultimate tailgater might build a cardboard or plywood façade of an old Spanish mission. This has several possibilities to be played on for names for your tailgate area—Mission Fiesta, Mission [insert your team's name here], or in the event your team is not doing well, Mission Impossible.

You'll also want a piñata. Again, this is an excellent opportunity to engage Spanish-American culture and make it your own. The piñata's origins are probably Chinese, and you can easily buy one whose recent origins are Chinese, too. You can purchase football and goalpost piñatas, or you can get one of your team's helmet or logo. If you're an ultimate tailgater with serious craft skills, you might want to make your own. Try fashioning your piñata in the form of the opposing team's mascot. This is appropriate if you wish to emphasize the beating and battering elements of the piñata game. A more sophisticated approach is to construct the piñata in the shape of your own mascot, so as to call attention to the virtues of your team—which, though whacked without mercy, nevertheless supplies sweetness and plenty to the crowd.

This last point is an obvious one, stated here only in the interest of clarity: truly ultimate fiesta tailgaters *will* have a live mariachi band. If this seems too much or beyond your means, reconsider. Mariachi bands are surprisingly easy to find, as even the most cursory Internet search reveals. Bands are available just about anywhere you're likely to attend a game, and many bands' repertoires are broader than you might think. One mariachi band out of Atlanta plays a stirring version of "Rocky Top," complete with the traditional peals of staccato trumpets demanded by serious fiesta tailgaters.

When thought through carefully, the fiesta tailgate will be memorable and it will inspire neighboring tailgaters to join in the spirit of your celebration rather than setting up a border guard.

CHRISTMAS TAILGATE

So often in the midst of the holiday season, we get caught up in the frenzy of playoffs and bowl games and need to find a way to stop and reflect on the holiday spirit. There's nothing like a Christmas tailgate party to delightfully combine the spirit of peace and good cheer while advancing our desire to see controlled and sanctioned violence on the field.

The Christmas tailgate works best when you bring the traditions of your home to the parking lot, albeit in somewhat modified fashion. Your aim should be to spread goodwill and team spirit. This festive feeling can be enhanced by a visit from Santa in a suit modified to refelct your team's colors. If you have a particular grudge against your opponent, your Santa might want to carry a large "Naughty Persons" list bearing the names of the opposing team's players and head coach. More elaborate lists can include their specific offenses against general goodness. Make sure your lettering is large enough to be read by viewers at home when you appear on TV.

As with all tailgate parties, the availability of electricity can have a real effect on what you can and can't accomplish (see **portable generators** on page 22). No electricity? Bring garlands, wreaths, and bows, and deck your temporary halls. A decorated tree adds wonderfully to the location. This does not need to be an elaborate twelve-foot-tall Douglas fir trimmed in sterling ornaments, but if you can arrange that, it will doubtless become tailgating folklore. Small trees can be used as centerpieces on your table. Larger trees, placed on the roof of your car, serve as a handy landmark for postgame revelers who have enjoyed too much cheer and need help finding their way back.

With electrical power available, ample possibilities open up. Holiday lights are an obvious nice touch. Simply string them around the edges of your tent or arrange them to spell out a cheerful holiday message of encouragement to your team.

Few tailgates beg more for music. At the very least, supply appropriate seasonal music to set the mood. Sing carols. If you and your friends sing well, consider a PA system and invite neighboring tailgaters to join in. If your neighbors don't like your singing, stop or they might help you stop. In the event this happens, please refer to the entry on **first-aid kits** (pages 28–29).

For the ultimate tailgater, more elaborate festivities will require an artificial fireplace and the construction of a hearth. An electric fireplace with a simulated flame always impresses, and few things make the parking lot cozier. Reindeer—real or artificial—can cause clutter, but having as many as nine lends a sense of authenticity to the visit from your team-specific Santa. Be creative. In some areas you might find it entirely appropriate to substitute your team's mascot for Santa's reindeer. Display eight jaguars or bears pulling a sleigh, for example. Picture the gleam in the eyes of passing children as they behold your Rudolph the Red-Nosed Raven . . . or Dolphin . . . or Bronco. Admittedly, some teams are at a disadvantage at times like this. The Red-Nosed Brown, for instance, is probably too abstract for the effect you seek. Work with the options available to you and make the most of them.

The ultimate tailgater might want to try recreating Santa's workshop in a little more detail by including elves. If you can bring children dressed in funny little outfits who can sit about making toys, your tailgate may achieve mythic proportions. This is also a way to involve your whole family in a tailgate while celebrating the season.

Also think about holding a gift exchange with each other or with your parking-lot neighbors, using gifts that celebrate your team. It's usually a good idea to put a price limit on these exchanges to keep everyone feeling the holiday cheer.

LUAU TAILGATE

The luau tailgate offers tremendous possibilities. Above all, it is an occasion for new ways to approach barbecue, and it can easily be expanded to include new experiences in your game-day wardrobe, beverages, and decorations—not to mention the opportunities to sing a new team fight song.

Luau is the Hawaiian word for the leaves of the *kalo* or *taro* plant, the root of which is mashed to make traditional *poi*, while the leaves are used to wrap any number of foods for steaming. The heavy use of the leaves has been associated so much with the traditional Hawaiian and Polynesian gatherings of communal thanksgiving that their name has come to be applied to the gatherings themselves. Add to your luau a specific theme of thanks: for friends, for your team's current standing, for whatever you like. In the event your team wins, you might wish to recall the ancient Polynesian tradition of the luau as a sign of thanks for victory in battle and continue your themed celebration after the game has ended.

There are a couple of points to consider as you begin planning your luau tailgate. First of all, you're going to need a conch shell or at least something similar that announces your festivity and makes a joyful noise. Air horns make poor substitutes for conch shells, but they have been used for this purpose.
The second point concerns the *imu*, which is the traditional pit oven used for roasting your pig. In most cases, you should forego the *imu*. There is no sense going to jail in a grass skirt and flower print shirt because you couldn't get the police to share your enthusiasm for digging through the blacktop to bury and roast your pig. Instead, hang a sign on your grill insisting that today it will be referred to as your *imu*, and don't dig any holes.

With these points out of the way, the rest is all a matter of just how ultimate you want your tailgate to be. Leis are absolutely essential and can be ordered or made in your team's colors. Real flowers are never wrong, but no one will be too upset if the flowers are fake. As for music, don't settle for Don Ho. Nothing against Mr. Ho, who surely deserves a wider reputation for excellence, but you should use this opportunity to dig into the rich trove of Polynesian and Hawaiian music for a little variety. On the other hand, if you own a ukulele, don't forget to bring it and play it if you can. Tiki lights are a good idea, too, if they fit your choice of decorations and if you have the means of powering them. They offer a safer alternative to the much more impressive and traditional open-flame torches not allowed by most stadiums (check the Resources section to see if your stadium allows open flames).

You should incorporate traditional Polynesian and Hawaiian dress into your tailgate. Grass skirts are fine in warm weather, but they can just as easily be worn over heavy clothing at your mid-winter luau. The same can be said of Hawaiian print shirts: wear them alone in warm weather or over heavier clothing when the temperature drops.

Before leaving your tailgate to head into the stadium, you might wish to sing a traditional chant from Maui to build your spirit. Of course, you're going to want to change a few words. Here's one song, with an English translation, that Hawaiians would traditionally sing:

'A'ohe mea like me Maui loa,	None other can compare with great Maui,
Ke kuahiwi 'oi kekakela o Lihau,	With its excellent mountain Lihau,
Ua ka 'a ia laki ia Maui apau.	All the luck has rolled forth on Maui.
Nani Lauhaina I ka'u'ike.	Beautiful is Lahaina to my estimation.

You can modify it to suit your team. Using the Indianapolis Colts as an example, what you wind up with is something like:

'A'ohe mea like me loa Indianapolis Colts,	None other can compare with the great Indianapolis Colts,
Ke kuahiwi 'oi kekakela o Tupe Peko,	With its excellent mountain Tupe Peko,
Ua ka 'a ia laki ia Indianapolis Colts apau.	All the luck has rolled forth on the Indianapolis Colts.
Nani Peyton Manning I ka'u'ike.	Beautiful is Peyton Manning to my estimation.

OKTOBERFEST TAILGATE

Tailgating is about many things. Oktoberfest is as well, but—with apologies to knockwurst and sauerkraut—the Oktoberfest tailgate is mostly about the beer. We say mostly because there ought to be room reserved on your tables and tailgates for some fine Bavarian fare (more on that in a minute). Tap your inner *braumeister*: create your own *biergarten* behind the car or, if at all possible, under the tent—and in so doing pour forth all your southern German and northern Alpine charm.

This party began in Munich in 1810, when Bavaria's King Joseph Maximilian celebrated the marriage of his son Ludwig to the princess Theresa of Saxonie. The little get-together went over so well that they did it again the following year, and the *volk* have returned annually in ever-increasing numbers. Royal wedding anniversaries aside, there's another good reason for this.

October happens to be a splendid month for beer. Real Oktoberfest beer is Märzen lager, beer brewed in March and allowed to mellow and ferment until it transforms into a variety of puckishly effervescent, delightfully crisp, deliciously redolent brews that look and taste like autumn in a glass.

The ultimate tailgater uses this Bavarian heritage to enhance the feel of the tailgate. Use a German-sounding team or player-inspired title to name your tailgate area. In Arizona you might choose something like Der Kardinalhaus. The possibilities are nearly endless.

The original Munich celebration was held on what is still called the Wiesen—short for the Theresienwiese, or Theresa's Field, in honor of Prince Ludwig's bride. Take that and work with it. A large banner in Gothic letters announcing your tailgate site as the Chiefswiese provides a sense of authenticity to your function.

Open your Oktoberfest tailgate with flair. Begin with the traditional cry of Munich's Mayor: "*O'zapft is!*" ("The keg is tapped!") This great proclamation has more authority behind it if you have actually just hammered a spigot into an oak barrel and filled your mug to the rim. If that cannot be arranged, give the cry anyway and pop a top. The phrase can certainly be used and appreciated symbolically.

Considering the size of most stadium parking spots, you will need to scale down the original festival from its collection of twelve colossal tents, each with its own beer, to twelve (or fewer in the interest of social responsibility) beer stations around your table. Make this tailgate a potluck affair: invite everyone to bring a different beer and award prizes. Perhaps the winner can take home a new pair of *lederhosen* or a charming *dirndl*. Runners-up might receive a glockenspiel or cuckoo clock. Be creative.

While the tapping of the keg (or opening of the bottle) kicks off your Oktoberfest tailgate, and there's no question it's the beer that has helped make Oktoberfest one of the biggest parties in the world each year, you will want to maintain the integrity of your Oktoberfest tailgate with the menu. That means leave your burgers in the refrigerator this week. In their place: bratwurst.

Some quick history. Germany has always found itself blessed with fertile terrain and ample water. This translates into good grazing country and a great place to raise beef and dairy cattle, sheep, and pigs. Fast-forward to today: simple but substantial food is the main characteristic of the German menu. Sauerkraut is still a hit, of course, as is the plethora of sausages (or wurst). You'll want to line your grill with the latter. As for side items, don't forget German dumplings or potato salad. And the ultimate Oktoberfest tailgate chef will want to roll out some Soft Pretzels to help stomachs soak up all the beer (see page 118 for that recipe).

Anyone who's ever been to an Oktoberfest celebration—or a German bar— knows there's one more important element to a successful Oktoberfest tailgate: "The Chicken Dance." While it's now known as "The Chicken Dance," when Werner Thomas wrote the tune in the 1970s he called it "Der Ententanz," which translates to "The Duck Dance." This is good news for Oregon fans: they can keep the original name for their tailgate. During the past three decades this song has had its greatest run of popularity in the United States. It has also been referred to as "Dance Little Bird," so fans of other feathered mascots can properly lay claim to "The Cardinal Dance," "The Eagle Dance," "The Gamecock Dance," and many others as they flap their wings and shake their tail feathers.

If by some slim chance you don't own a copy of "The Chicken Dance," a simple Google search will get you what you need. Many versions are available from the traditional to pop to children's versions. So there's no excuse to skip this Oktoberfest ritual.

Only the Franco-Prussian War, two world wars, and an 1873 cholera epidemic have halted the Oktoberfest in Munich. One Oktoberfest tailgate will almost inevitably lead to more, and you may quickly find yourself hosting this as an annual event. You can pull this off with some planning and hard work. People will flock to your Parkplatzwiese. So chances are, if you've done it right, your Oktoberfest tailgate will become a ritual, too.

HALLOWEEN TAILGATE

If hosting, or even attending, tailgate parties with a theme daunts you (perhaps you don't trust your creative powers?), here is the tailgate theme with which to get started. Almost anyone can work with Halloween. Supplies, from the ubiquitous plastic spider ring to the more elaborate house of horror props, are easy to find. Costumes of every description are readily available. In fact, how to throw a Halloween party is probably so clear to you already, we will not deal in depth here with the basic elements.

As with any game-day get-together, the Halloween tailgate's level of success is contingent on your ability to adapt and apply several basic key ingredients. Team-specific horror is what you're after here. You can never go wrong with the most familiar assortment of costumes—witches, psychopathic killers, any number of recognizable monsters from movies or myth. Or, most simple of all, and charming in its own way, is the formless sheet-over-the-head ghost costume with large eye-hole cutouts. As always, more thought and effort can produce, well, more, and help make your tailgate an affair to be remembered by your guests and everyone who passes by.

For some fans simply coming dressed to support their tem is costume enough. If this is not your style, consider using needle and thread to make a costume that pays homage to your favorite team, especially if the team mascot lends itself to a Halloween motif. In Denver you might consider going as a bronco. In Cincinnati a tiger. At California-Irvine, an anteater could be fun. If your team is having a fine year after a bad spell, use that to your advantage. A nice big banner with gory or spooky lettering boldly declaring your team "Back from the Dead" can be thematic, potentially creepy, and serve to offer enthusiastic encouragement.

The possibilities of attending as a ghoulish cheerleader—or with your friends as an entire cheerleading squad of the damned—are frightfully exciting. If you or your friends need some help coming up with original costumes, or if you just want to make your Halloween tailgate more unique, go with a sub-theme. For example, have everyone come as their favorite penalty. Offensive holding could be provocative. Illegal motion, the same. Just don't be the one called for delay of game.

For some basic decorations, try constructing a graveyard of tombstones with the names of the opposing team's players. Normally, this would be in poor taste, but Halloween provides a measure of freedom to be exploited. Not sure this is appropriate? Turn the tables on the idea and create a touching (yet still macabre) memorial graveyard scene with tombstones bearing the names of former members of your own team.

The ultimate tailgater will want to secure dry ice for the occasion. Used effectively, dry ice can work at either daytime or evening events to create the eerie atmosphere of mist creeping over the haunted moors or between the headstones—even if you are set up in row 17 of the Apple Area. At the very least, having a cooler with heavy vapors slowly rising from it and seeping down its sides will impress others and lend real credibility to your celebration.

If you do use dry ice, handle it with care. Wear hand protection whenever touching it. An oven mitt or thick folded towel will work. Proper ventilation is also imperative. Check out www.painenterprises.com/safetydryice.html for more information on handling dry ice.

Don't leave your food and drinks out of the thematic fun. Creating a Potion Punch (page 145) or offering someone a Zombie (page 159) makes the event that much more fun and allows you to stretch your creativity beyond the basic candy corn. Not that candy corn should lack a role in your tailgate. In fact, be sure to bring lots of candy for trick-or-treaters who amble by. A handful of candy in the bag of a little ghost or goblin goes a long way toward creating friendships with your neighbors. You might even want to create a Halloween trick-or-treat version of a scavenger hunt for your tailgate crew . . . replacing some of the items in the Football Scavenger Hunt (page 81) with things like vampires, horror movie characters, and jack-o-lanterns.

Speaking of jack-o-lanterns, the ultimate tailgater will want to have several on hand to set the mood and help light an evening tailgate. The ultimate tailgater's pumpkins will feature team mascots as well as the traditional devils, skeletons, and bats. If you need a refresher on carving techniques and tools, or need some patterns, log on to www.theultimatetailgater.com for links to some sites to help you.

Racing

Look across the parking lot at a NASCAR race and it won't take you long to
realize you're not in Kansas anymore. Unless you're at the Banquet 400.
Then you are in Kansas. But you get the point.

Tailgating at racing events takes on an entirely different atmosphere from
football games. NASCAR tailgates share many of the tools and gear of their
football cousins, but the spirit is definitely different.

For one thing, there's no home team. No home colors. Racing, of course,
doesn't pit two teams battling for four quarters. It pits dozens of teams
accelerating and drafting for hundreds of laps. Each NASCAR race has the
atmosphere of the Super Bowl, with RVs rolling in days in advance and fans
camping out. These are big events.

At "the Monster Mile" in Dover, Delaware, the two annual NASCAR races are
the largest sporting events in the state, drawing more than 170,000 spectators.
At the Daytona 500, the Super Bowl of Auto Racing, more than 60,000 people
fill the infield alone.

To find the best NASCAR tailgate parties in the country, we turned to Steve
McCormick, the NASCAR and racing guru for About.com. He tailgates at races
across the country and says these are the top five tailgate parties:

1. BRISTOL MOTOR SPEEDWAY

"Not only is the August race under the lights one of the best races on the
NASCAR schedule, it hosts the best tailgate party. These are some of the
friendliest fans on earth. You may not be able to get tickets, but if you do
you'll never have a hard time finding a great party."

2. LOWE'S MOTOR SPEEDWAY

"These fans are the most hardcore NASCAR fans on the planet. If you want
to get into an in-depth discussion about the sport, then you need to be in

Charlotte for the 600, and with the three-day Memorial Day holiday they have extra time to party."

3. INDIANAPOLIS MOTOR SPEEDWAY

"Take the NASCAR crowd, add in the old Indy 500 crowd, and you've got a recipe for some serious partying."

4. POCONO RACEWAY

"An unusual choice for anyone who has never been there. I don't know if it's the poor sightlines for the fans, unbearable traffic jams, lack of other entertainment, or what, but Pocono hosts a surprisingly rocking bash twice a year."

5. INFINEON RACEWAY

"Tailgating in Sonoma features quite a mix of race fans. You get the wine-and-cheese crowd rubbing elbows with NASCAR's traditional blue-collar set. It makes for a good time all around."

The thing that makes racing tailgaters special is that they hang out with each other for so long. Football tailgaters are in and out in a day. NASCAR tailgaters roll in on Thursday or Friday and don't head home until Sunday.

"The atmosphere is more like camping," Steve says. "You'll see people playing horseshoes and things like that. People are also friendlier at NASCAR tailgates and more open to being approached and having you hang out by their fire for an hour sharing a beer. There's a feeling that it is unique and special, even though the sport has exploded."

And it has exploded . . . doubling in attendance since 1990. This has made the tailgates bigger and added to the feeling of community, even though you have fans wearing the colors of more than forty different teams and drivers.

"There may not be any 'Give me a big hug, you fellow Steelers fan,' but there's a lot of 'Your guy wrecked my guy last week and he'll pay for it this week,'" Steve explains. "It's friendly, not antagonistic, and even though you may see each other only once a year, great friendships are born. After all, you camped out with them for three days."

How does this campout feeling translate to the food? It adds to the diversity. "You see a good bit of the million-dollar mobile homes cooking lobster and stuff like that," Steve reports. "Then in the next row, you have people camped out in tents eating hot dogs. It's more camping food than tailgating food."

Another distinction at NASCAR races: tailgaters and fans can listen in on the drivers. All you need is a scanner to pick up the radio frequencies, and then you can hear the drivers talking with their crews. You can buy a frequency sheet at the race for about $8. You can also subscribe to services that will send you lists updated weekly (some of the drivers change their radio frequencies race-to-race). But we suggest logging on to www.racefreqs.com, which has free updated lists for NASCAR Series races and others.

If you aren't at the race and don't live within a few miles of the track, you can still listen in on the races with Nextel Track Pass from www.NASCAR.com. There is a fee for this service, but it also includes a number of other features.

Most people will tell you that if there's one drawback to tailgating, it's the amount of time it takes. Depending on where you are, and with whom, it can take up just about all day. For many, though, that's the point. However, for some spouses or friends who come along for the game, passing the time can be a problem.

But don't look at those hours before the game, or the time spent waiting for the parking-lot traffic to clear, as an obstacle to having a good time. They aren't. They're an opportunity to have even more fun.

There's no reason pools and games should be shelved away and brought out only for collegiate bowl season or the Super Bowl. These activities help make the game more exciting and can also help you make friends around the parking lot.

There are a couple of keys to a good tailgating game. The first is that it can be played by any number of people. If the size of your tailgate fluctuates from week to week, you want to be able to accommodate the changing numbers. You also want to be able to add other tailgaters in your area to the game. It's the neighborly thing to do; plus you never know if you'll make a new business contact or get a date this way (not with the business contact, of course).

The second key is that the game is simple to understand. While knowledge of football or racing statistics and trivia may be helpful in the game, it should never be required. Tailgating is for everyone from the casual to the hardcore fan.

These pools and games will get you started. You'll find more at www.theultimatetailgater.com. You can also download proposition pool player forms and crossword puzzles from the Web site to take to your tailgate.

Two final words before you start having fun: be creative. Change up the rules some. Create your own games. Play different games each week. It will make your tailgate party more exciting and have folks eager to pack up the car and return to the stadium for the next game.

Pools have a simple premise: people make predictions before the game and the play on the field determines the winner. It will help if you do your homework to find out who's playing well and what the "experts" are saying. But, just like that fumble on the one or the pass picked off in the end zone, even a novice has a good chance of winning.

GRIDIRON PROPOSITION POOL (College and pro football)

Number of players: Two or more.
To win: Earn the most points by correctly predicting the events of the game.
Duration: One game.

Those with more knowledge of the strengths and weaknesses of the teams playing might believe they have the upper hand, but because the outcome of some events can be determined by luck or subjective opinion (the replay option can turn the tide), even the casual fan can win.

Score two points for each correct prediction; the most points wins.

Winning team   _____

First team to score   _____

A safety will be scored   ❏ Yes   ❏ No

A replay will overturn a call*   ❏ Yes   ❏ No

Points scored in the last
2 minutes of the first half   ❏ Yes   ❏ No

* For most college games, exclude this event since it isn't applicable.

Field goal more than 45 yards   ❏ Yes   ❏ No

A player will rush for more
than 100 yards   ❏ Yes   ❏ No

Blocked FG or punt   ❏ Yes   ❏ No

Successful 2-point conversion   ❏ Yes   ❏ No

Defensive unit scores TD   ❏ Yes   ❏ No

Special teams scores TD   ❏ Yes   ❏ No

Fake field goal   ❏ Yes   ❏ No

QB passes for more than 300 yards   ❏ Yes   ❏ No

Tie breaker #1:
Total points (winner closest without going over)   _____

Tie breaker #2:
Running time of the National Anthem   _____
(The pool organizer will need to time the National Anthem in case it decides the winner.)

PICK SIX (Pro football)

Number of players: Two or more.

To win: Be the first player to correctly predict the winner of all six of the six pro football games you have selected.

Duration: The game's organizer can have this pool last as briefly as one week to as long as the full season.

To play this game, each participant picks six NFL games for the week and predicts the winner of each. The first to correctly predict all six wins the pool. If no one wins, no one is eliminated; everyone can play until there's a winner.

If someone wins Pick Six before the scheduled end of the pool, just get everyone together and start over for the rest of the season. If no one has won by the end of the season, the NFL playoffs become the Pick Six playoffs. Take the six best performers from the regular season (you will want to keep track of everyone's weekly record) and have them play through the playoffs. This playoff pool will try to pick the correct winner for all of that week's games, since the pool of teams and games shrinks each week and there are no longer six from which to choose.

If no one wins at all, and you've collected money for your pool where it's legal, you can return the money to the participants. However, our suggestion is to end the game after the conference championships, take the funds, and throw a Super Bowl party for everyone.

TOP-TEN POOL (College football)

Number of players: Two or more.

To win: Earn the most points by correctly predicting which teams will be
     in the top-ten polls most often during the season.

Duration: The college football season.

To play this game, everyone at your first tailgate of the season (it's best to start this game no later than the first game of the year) will write down the ten Division I-A teams he or she believes will spend the most weeks in the top ten of the polls. The game's organizer will determine which national poll (AP, USA Today/ESPN, etc.) will be used.

Each week a player gets ten points for each week one of his or her teams is ranked number 1, nine points for each week his or her team is ranked number 2, etc. At the end of the season if there is a tie, the first tie breaker would be the most number 1's garnered by the player's team, then the most number 2's, and so on until the tie is broken.

NASCAR KENO (Racing)

Number of players: Between two and ten.

To win: Match your number most often with the last digit of the lap leader for each segment.

Duration: One race

This is a simple game to play and also a game that will have participants cheering for and against their favorite drivers at certain points of the race.

Prior to the race, each player draws a number between zero and nine from a hat. The participant gets one point for each ten-lap segment his or her number matches the last digit of the lap leader's car number. The checkered flag is the final segment, and the player with the most points wins. (Obviously, the game's more fun with ten players than with two since there's a chance that with fewer players no one will win.)

THE CHECKERED FLAG PROPOSITION POOL (Racing)

Number of players: Two or more.

To win: Earn the most points by correctly predicting the events of the race.

Duration: One race.

While knowledge of racing can be helpful with this pool, just as often, a wreck or a bad pit stop can quickly change the race's outcome.

Score two points for each correct prediction in questions 1–7, and the correct points from question 8; the most points wins.

Pole sitter leads at the end of Lap 1	❏ Yes	❏ No
Leader with 10 laps to go wins race	❏ Yes	❏ No
Margin of victory is less than 1 second	❏ Yes	❏ No
Winning driver leads the most laps	❏ Yes	❏ No
Cautions outnumber lap leaders	❏ Yes	❏ No
Pole sitter finishes in the top 5	❏ Yes	❏ No
The race ends under a caution flag	❏ Yes	❏ No

Select three drivers (in any order) and score five points if the race winner is among your selected drivers, three points if the second place finisher is one of your three, and one point if the third place finisher is in your trio.

Drivers:

1. _____ 2. _____ 3. _____

Tie breaker:

Finishing position of the pole sitter _____

"DOWN THE STRETCH" KENTUCKY DERBY PROPOSITION POOL (Horse racing)

Number of players: Two or more.

To win: Earn the most points by correctly predicting the events of the race.

Duration: One race.

In horse racing knowledge of the horses and past success can help you win.pools like these. Reading Magazines like *Bloodhorse* and *Thoroughbred Times* before the race may help you out.

Score two points for each correct prediction in questions 1–7, and the correct points from question 8; the most points wins.

Race-time favorite wins	❏ Yes	❏ No
Margin of victory under one length	❏ Yes	❏ No
Winning jockey has won before (since 1979 Derby)	❏ Yes	❏ No
Winning trainer has won before (since 1979 Derby)	❏ Yes	❏ No
Winning jockey's colors include red or blue	❏ Yes	❏ No
Winning horse foaled in Kentucky	❏ Yes	❏ No
Winning horse has name of ten letters or more	❏ Yes	❏ No

Select three horses (in any order) and score five points if the race winner is among your selected horses, three points if the second place finisher is one of your three, and one point if the third place finisher is in your trio.

Horses: 1. _____   Tie breaker:

2. _____   3. _____   Winning time of race _____

SCAVENGER HUNTS

We don't really picnic anymore in America. We tailgate. People from all walks of life find their way to the parking lot on game or race day. You never know who you'll meet. Or what your newfound acquaintances have with them. It's the latter fact that makes tailgate scavenger hunts so much fun.

The rules of the game are the same as they were when you were a kid scavenging around the neighborhood trying to complete your list before your sister finished hers. Only the stuff you're looking for has changed.

One of the wonderful things about scavenger hunts is the ability to keep them fresh by changing out the items on the list. That's why we've included a comprehensive list to get you started. Pick ten or twelve of the items and include them for your tailgate scavenger hunt.

To get started you'll want to select your items and prepare sheets for your teams. We suggest teams of two because it makes it easier to canvas the parking lot, and you won't have too many people running around asking tailgaters for the same things. Once everyone has arrived, hand out the sheets, tell everyone how much time they have (allow at least an hour because you know everyone will want to stop and talk with people, which is what tailgating is all about), and turn them loose. The first team that gets back to the tailgate with a completed list is the winner.

One other thing has changed since the scavenger hunts of your youth: technology. Make sure each team has a digital camera, since many of the items they're looking for are not things with which people will want to part . . . but they'll be thrilled to have you take a picture of their stuff.

FOOTBALL SCAVENGER HUNT

(Collect or take picture of items listed)

#9 jersey (use numbers for star players
  from home and visiting teams)
Adult with painted face
Card table
Celebrity
Chef hat
Cow bells
Deck of cards
Dog wearing a football jersey
Elvis impersonator
Face painter
Fan wearing a toga
Fan wearing headband
Football cake
Football hitch cover
Football kicking tee
Football-shaped pasta
Football trophy
Former pro football player
Giant inflatable helmet
Golf club
Green Nerf football
Gridiron tablecloth
Guitar
Hard hat with team logo
Home team blanket
Home team bottle opener
Home team coffee mug
Home team cooking apron
Home team folding chairs
Home team license plate
Home team logo bus
Home team logo Frisbee
Home team painted grill
Inflatable furniture

Man with white beard who looks like Santa
Person with wild/colored wig
Picture of dumbest hat
Picture of home team QB
Picture of visiting team QB
Player-autographed football
Player-autographed helmet
Player-autographed jersey
Policeman with football
Professional athlete
Red, white, and blue balloons together
Stuffed animal football mascot
Styrofoam brick
Team cheerleader
  (real one, not fan dressed in outfit)
Team helmet piñata
Team logo cigar cutter
Team logo hat with multiple
  player autographs
Team mascot (real one, not fan in costume)
Toddler in cheerleading outfit
Toddler in helmet
Toddler with football
Toddler with painted face
Twins wearing identical team outfits
Visiting team blanket
Visiting team bottle opener
Visiting team coffee mug
Visiting team cooking apron
Visiting team folding chairs
Visiting team license plate
Visiting team logo bus
Visiting team logo Frisbee
Visiting team painted grill
Whistle

RACING SCAVENGER HUNT

(Collect or take picture of items listed)

#20 hitch cover
#24 coffee mug
#3 coffee mug
#3 earrings
#3 hat
#3 hitch cover
#8 coffee mug
#9 hat
#97 jacket
Adult with face painted
Autographed picture of driver
Beer can with NASCAR driver/team on it
Black cowboy hat
Brooke and Jeff Gordon picture (together)
Cake shaped as speedway
Celebrity
Checkered flag
Checkered flag napkins
Checkered flag on a lighter
Checkered flag pattern sneakers
Checkered flag seat cushion
Checkered flag shirt
Checkered flag tablecloth
Clothing item with multiple driver
  autographs
Custom-painted gas grill
Dog wearing NASCAR collar
Driver hat autographed by the driver
Elvis impersonator
Former driver
Ford racing flag
Jeff Gordon pen or pencil
Kurt Busch 2004 Nextel Cup Champion Poster
License plate that says "The King"
Map of track
NASCAR beanbag
NASCAR belt buckle

NASCAR bottle opener
NASCAR cooler
NASCAR deck of cards
NASCAR driver clock
NASCAR driver pet food bowl
NASCAR fans with favorite
  bag of beef jerky
NASCAR Frisbee
NASCAR hard hat
NASCAR hockey shirt
NASCAR lighter
NASCAR mug
NASCAR official Tabasco sauce
NASCAR piñata
NASCAR salt and pepper shakers
NASCAR schedule T-shirt
NASCAR tailgate table
NASCAR tattoo (real one, not temporary)
Person wearing both #18 and #44 clothing
Person wearing car number earrings
Person with a car number painted
  on his chest
Picture of Dale and Dale Jr. together
Picture of driver in golf cart
Picture of Lil' E with no baseball hat on
Picture of Tom Cruise
Professional athlete
Race—car—shaped grill
Racing gear with clock attached
Red balloons
Remote control car
Richard Petty bobble head
Someone from a foreign country
  (they must have passport)
STP key chain
Toddler in cool-looking shades
Toddler with face painted

CROSSWORD PUZZLES

If you really want to test your knowledge of the sport, a crossword puzzle will do it. These test not only your football or racing knowledge, but your language skills, too.

These crossword puzzles are designed to be completed alone or in teams. You may want to divide your tailgate crew into teams of two to four and see who can finish the grid first. Or you may want to take yours to your chair by the grill and show everyone how smart you are.

You'll find printable versions of these puzzles and others at www.theultimatetailgater.com.

NFL

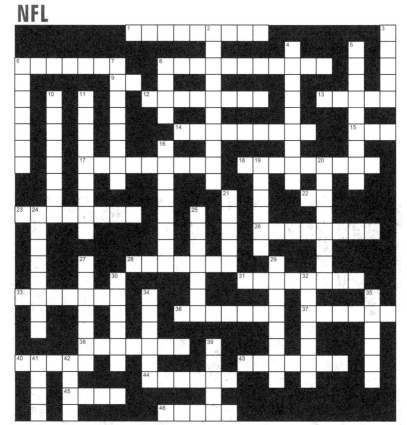

solution on page 219

DOWN

2. Host to most number of Super Bowls
3. Only San Diego Charger to have his number retired
4. Oldest continuing team in professional football
5. Most turnovers in one game (by both teams)
6. Team first known as the Steers
7. Super Bowl X winner
8. The 12th man
10. Trophy coach
11. Most consecutive games lost (Tampa Bay, 1976–1977)
16. Attempted record 650 FGs in career
19. Former Dallas Texans
20. Cowboys #12
21. Super Bowl I & II MVP
24. First known as the Boston Braves
25. Parcell's nickname
27. Team first sponsored by the Indian Packing Company
29. Played record 282 consecutive games
30. The Bus
32. Formation
34. Two points
35. Mean Joe _____
39. Super Bowl XXX MVP
41. Hall of Fame state
42. Carpet

ACROSS

1. Walter Payton
6. Most Super Bowl appearances
8. In 1906 this play became legal
9. Cowboys RB initial
12. Super Bowl XXV MVP
13. Chargers' wind
14. St. Louis Rams' original city
15. First and _____
17. Vikings rookie QB who won franchise debut
18. In 2002 set record for longest return of a missed FG (107 yards)
22. The Bald Eagle
23. Football field
26. Blocking back
28. Randy White nickname
31. Steelers' 1970 #1 pick
33. Music City _____
36. Super Bowl winner
37. Former Houston team
38. Team briefly known as the Señors
40. Super Bowl V winner
43. Owns team record for most yards gained in one season (7,075)
44. Penalty flag color
45. Owns record for most career TD's (205)
46. 49ers' lefty QB

COLLEGE FOOTBALL

solution on page 220

2. Holds both the game and the season records for the most points scored and passed for in a game
3. Former Nebraska coach
4. BC Heisman winner
6. Grambling legend
7. Stanford mascot
8. The Bear
10. Namath college
12. Michigan nickname
13. 1996 National Champions
16. Saban coached these Tigers
18. Happy Valley legend
19. Rutgers home state
20. Duck and Dillard universities share this nickname
21. Florida ex-coach
22. Maryland conference
24. Vols' stadium
28. Only Heisman repeat
32. David Neill gained a freshman record 582 yards in one game (1198) playing for the Wolf Pack
33. Texas's long-horned mascot
34. Georgia abbreviation
35. Atlanta's bowl game

ACROSS

1. When QB tackled behind the line
5. Home of the Rose Bowl
9. 1956 Heisman winner
11. Pitt mascot
14. Holtz coached here
15. Standford standout QB
17. 2005 Orange Bowl victor
22. Cal-Irvine mascot
23. Owns record for most yards rushed for in one game (406)
25. Vandy conference
26. 1996 Heisman winner
27. ND's famous backfield
29. 2000 National Champions
30. 1981 Heisman winner
31. Owns record for most yards rushed for in one quarter (222)
33. Home of the blue turf
36. Galloping Ghost
37. Long pass
38. Division III Championship _____ Bowl

NASCAR

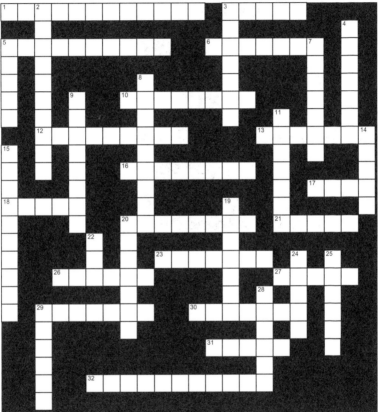

solution on page 221

2. Too tough to tame
3. Won Daytona in 1976
4. The Birthplace of Speed
5. Monster Mile
7. Dollar Bill
8. Tony Stewart sponsor
9. Won Championship in 1992
11. First brother team to start 1-2 at Daytona
14. Holds longest margin of victory at Daytona
15. Won Championship in 1976
19. World's Fastest Half Mile
20. Mr. Excitement
22. #43 sponsor
24. Dale's dad
25. Commander in Chief to watch Petty win #200
28. Father of NASCAR
29. Gordon ex

ACROSS

1. The Brickyard
3. 200 wins
5. Lady in Black
6. The Iceman
10. First woman to enter a NASCAR event
12. "The fastest"
13. White flag
16. Coach Gibbs's team
17. Older driver at inaugural Brickyard
18. Penalty flag color
20. Brand new tires
21. Dale Jr. car

23. Oldest driver to win Daytona
26. Gordon sponsor
27. First driver to break 200 mph
29. Tire bubble
30. Won Championships in 1981
31. 2004 Rookie of the Year
32. Winner's Circle

The Commissioner of Tailgating

Did you hear the one about the guy from New Orleans who spends football season on the road visiting every NFL stadium each year? And along the way he hits dozens of colleges. And all he does is tailgate. If so, you've heard about the Commissioner of Tailgating. Oh, you haven't heard of him either? "It was a secret election," says the Commissioner. "More than fifty million ballots were cast. I collected ballots from tailgaters across the country; there was only one ballot box. It was a unanimous decision."

A unanimous decision for Joe Cahn, the Commissioner of Tailgating. "It was between me and Richard Simmons," Cahn explains. "But he wanted people to exercise. I was the eating candidate."

And the Commissioner does a lot of that in parking lots from Oregon to Maine. In 1996 Cahn sold his New Orleans School of Cooking and decided to try his hand at a cooking show. The idea was to tailgate at every NFL stadium in one season. The show hasn't hit the air, but Cahn's been hitting the road ever since.

He hasn't always been the Commissioner of Tailgating. That title came in 1997. Before that he was the King of Tailgating. Why the change? "Kings can be overthrown. Commissioners are forever."

THE COMMISSIONER'S WISDOM FROM THE ROAD
- Tailgating is part of the fiber of the game-day experience.
- It's not about the number of tailgaters at a stadium, it's about participating. "When you go to Kansas City, you know you're in Kansas City—it's a sea of red!"
- While food is a main ingredient of the tailgate, food doesn't make the party. "Your friends make the party. When you're standing around laughing with your friends, hot dogs taste great."
- Attitude is key to a successful tailgate. "A tailgate is a special place where

the only stranger is the person you haven't said 'hello' to yet. And wear your team's colors—that's very important."

THE COMMISSIONER'S TOP TAILGATES
NFL
Buffalo, Green Bay, Kansas City, New England

College

SEC, Big 10, and Big 12 conference schools
Honorable mention: University of Washington
("It's great because of all the boats . . .
it's Sterngating!")

THE COMMISSIONER'S TOP-TEN TAILGATING MISTAKES

1. Getting drunk
2. Not having a checklist and forgetting things*
3. Not bringing trash bags and not cleaning up after your tailgate
4. Not bringing enough food
5. Not bringing enough ice
6. Not treating visitors with courtesy just because they're wearing the colors of the opposing team
7. Using obscenity—verbally and by means of clothing, like wearing a T-shirt insulting your opponent rather than supporting your team
8. Not being dressed properly for the weather
9. Leaving your radio, TV, or other item on and running down your car battery
10. Not having jumper cables to help people who leave their radio, TV, or other item on and run down their car battery

*You'll find a complete checklist on pages 95–96.

Good Sports—Tailgating Etiquette

The dictionary defines *sportsmanship* as "conduct (such as fairness, respect for one's opponent, and graciousness in winning or losing) becoming to one participating in a sport." That also goes for the sport of tailgating.

Fans in the parking lot, just like players on the field, should employ sportsmanlike conduct. Too often, manners in and around sporting events take a backseat to a few foul-mouthed fantasy coaches and party animals who are in their own little world. Some fans believe they are bigger than the game, that it's their right as a ticket holder to act like a moron.

However, practicing proper tailgating etiquette and conducting yourself with good manners at a tailgate can lead to lifetime friendships and might even get you invited to a few more games down the road. It really does pay to be a good sport.

So how do good sports act?

- Good sports never take up more space than needed while tailgating.

- Good sports pay, or at least offer to pay, for parking and tolls if the tailgate host is driving.

- Good sports never throw the ball around when cars are still parking nearby.

- Good sports don't wear shirts that contain foul language. They'll only end up embarrassing themselves—especially when children are present.

- Good sports are able to draw the line between good-natured ribbing and obnoxious behavior.

- Good sports are aware of which way the wind is blowing their cigar or grill smoke.

- Good sports always apologize in a nice manner after knocking over a tableful of food with an incomplete pass or a Frisbee.

- Good sports try not to spend too much time on their cell phones. Enjoy the people you are with.

- Good sports offer food and drink to tailgate neighbors.

- Good sports don't throw food at people.

- Good sports say "please" and "thank you."

- Good sports don't let their pets run loose.

- Good sports never use gas and flames to impress others.

- Good sports realize when the stereo volume may be a little much.

- Good sports never complain about seats that are a gift.

- Good sports respect others and use appropriate language.

- Good sports show manners to their opponent's fans and act sportsmanlike after the results of the game are final.

- Good sports thank the tailgate host for the time spent preparing the food.

- Good sports leave the tailgate venue the way they found it. Everybody cleans up.

- Good sports don't drive drunk.

Planning Your Tailgate

he novelist Mark Caine (perhaps best known for his book *S-Man*), once said, "Meticulous planning will enable everything a man does to appear spontaneous." A good lesson for the ultimate tailgater.

Tailgating should be fun and spontaneous. But you don't want to spontaneously run out of ice. Or drinks. Or food.

As you've read in these pages, good planning is the key to good tailgating. We've given you tips and ideas for how to plan your tailgate and what you need to load into the car. But we want to make it simple for you; after all, that's the point of a handbook. So we've created The Ultimate Tailgater's Checklist and The Ultimate Tailgater's Planning Guide. You can use the ones in the book or download them from www.theultimatetailgater.com. Either way, if you make them a part of your weekend ritual, you'll find yourself having more spontaneous fun.

ULTIMATE TAILGATER'S CHECKLIST

FOR YOUR VEHICLE
- ❑ Car door de-icer
- ❑ Car flags
- ❑ First-aid kit
- ❑ Fix-A-Flat (or similar brand)
- ❑ Flare
- ❑ Jumper cables
- ❑ Rags
- ❑ Water
- ❑ Check the fluids before you leave for the game

TO HAVE FOR PREGAME
- ❑ Antacid
- ❑ Ash container
- ❑ Aspirin
- ❑ Binoculars
- ❑ Blanket
- ❑ Camera
- ❑ Decorations
- ❑ Extension cords
- ❑ Face paint
- ❑ Food
- ❑ Football/Frisbee
- ❑ Gum

- ❏ Insulated drink holders
- ❏ Lighter/matches
- ❏ Moist towelettes
- ❏ Paper towels
- ❏ Rain/snow/sun gear
- ❏ Radio
- ❏ Seat cushions
- ❏ Toilet paper (you only think it's silly until you're trapped in a porta-potty that has run out)
- ❏ Toothpicks
- ❏ Towels
- ❏ TV with AC adapter
- ❏ Umbrella
- ❏ Visine
- ❏ Water, lots of water, for washing hands, for cooking, for cleanup, and even for drinking

COOKING AND SERVING TOOLS

- ❏ Aluminum foil
- ❏ Basting brush
- ❏ Bottle opener
- ❏ Bowls/cups/plates
- ❏ Chairs
- ❏ Coolers
- ❏ Corkscrew
- ❏ Garbage bags
- ❏ Grill/charcoal/fire-start fluid
- ❏ Ice
- ❏ Ketchup
- ❏ Kitchen knives
- ❏ Latex gloves
- ❏ Mustard
- ❏ Napkins
- ❏ Other condiments
- ❏ Pots/pans
- ❏ Paperweights (to keep those napkins from blowing away)
- ❏ Serving spoons/forks
- ❏ Spatula/tongs
- ❏ Salt and pepper
- ❏ Tables for serving/eating/food prep
- ❏ Utensils

BEFORE HEADING INTO THE GAME, DON'T FORGET . . .

- ❏ Charcoal extinguished and away from vehicles and flammables
- ❏ Clean up
- ❏ Keys with you
- ❏ Lock your car
- ❏ Note your parking space location
- ❏ Turn off car
- ❏ Your tickets

ULTIMATE TAILGATER'S PLANNING GUIDE

TWO WEEKS OUT

If you tailgate with a large group, decide who will be bringing which items. Go ahead and divvy up the food, the serving items, the drinks and coolers.

ONE WEEK OUT

If you are a gas grill user, make sure you have enough propane.

Prepare all foods that can be made several days ahead.

DAY/EVENING BEFORE

Prepare all food items that can be prepared one day ahead.

Start marinating any meats you plan to take to the game.

Pack things such as decorations, "kitchen" set-up items, utensils

(You can pack more carefully the night before when you aren't rushed).

Charge up your cell phone.

Review your food recipes and make sure you have all the ingredients.

Check your first-aid kit to make sure it is stocked (see list of items on page 29).

DAY OF GAME

Make sure your car has all the items on the For Your Vehicle checklist (see page 95). Pack all perishable food into coolers to make sure it will travel safely.

Make sure you have the game tickets. Load up your car and, if you have a long way to travel, make sure your coolers won't be in the sun.

Review checklists of items you'll need to take to the game (see pages 95–96). Load up your family and friends.

Tailgating Cookbook

What's a tailgate party without food and drinks in the hands of fans? It's certainly not an ultimate tailgate party. In fact, it's really not a party at all.

It's not so much *what* you eat and drink that's important at your tailgate, but that you have *something* and enough of it for all of your guests. And don't forget to plan for the time after the game when you will want to snack while waiting for the traffic to clear. That's the perfect time for some Peanut Butter Swirl Brownies (page 137).

Whether you plan a basic tailgate or something grander, we've collected some food and drink recipes to satisfy most any tailgater. We've included main dishes and sides, snacks and desserts. You'll also find delicious drinks, including nonalcoholic ones for all ages.

But these aren't all the recipes from our pantry. We'll rotate additional food and drink recipes throughout the season at www.theultimatetailgater.com.

 Recipes with this icon are great to make at home and bring with you to your tailgate.

FOOD INDEX

Joe's Jambalaya

1½ pounds boneless, skinless chicken breasts, cut into 1-inch pieces

Salt

Ground black pepper

¼ cup vegetable oil

1½ pounds sausage cut in ¼-inch pieces

4 cups chopped onion

2 cups chopped celery

2 cups chopped green bell pepper

1 tablespoon minced garlic

5 cups chicken stock or water flavored with chicken bouillon

2 tablespoons seasoned salt

2 tablespoons Kitchen Bouquet (browning agent)

4 cups long grain rice

2 cups chopped green onions

Season the chicken with the salt and pepper. Brown the chicken in the hot oil in a large Dutch oven or stockpot over medium-high heat. Add the sausage and cook 5 to 7 minutes. Remove the chicken and the sausage from the pan. Add the onions, celery, green peppers, and garlic to the pan. Cook, stirring, for 7 to 10 minutes, or until the vegetables begin to soften. Stir in the chicken stock, the cooked chicken and sausage, the seasoned salt, and Kitchen Bouquet. Bring the contents to a boil. Add the rice and return to a boil. Cover the pot and reduce the heat to simmer. Cook for 10 minutes. Remove the cover and quickly turn the rice from top to bottom. Replace the cover and cook for 15 to 20 minutes more, or until the liquid is absorbed and the rice is tender. Stir in the green onions.

If using an electric stove, reduce cooking time by 3 to 4 minutes.

Makes 12 to 15 servings.

Teriyaki Chicken Kebabs

1½ pounds skinless, boneless chicken breasts

1 small bunch green onions, cut into 1-inch pieces

½ cup soy sauce

2 tablespoons sugar

1 teaspoon oil

1 teaspoon minced fresh ginger root

1 clove garlic, minced

Cut the chicken into 1½-inch pieces. Thread the chicken onto skewers, alternating with the green onion pieces. Place in a shallow baking dish. Combine the soy sauce, sugar, oil, ginger, and garlic. Mix well and pour over the skewers, coating the chicken evenly. Cover and refrigerate for 30 minutes.

Preheat the grill and place the skewers over medium-high heat. Grill for about 4 minutes; turn and brush with the remaining marinade. Grill an additional 4 minutes, or until done.

Makes 6 to 8 servings.

Garlic-Grilled Chicken Skewers

2 pounds boneless, skinless chicken breasts

1 cup salsa

2 tablespoons vegetable oil

1 tablespoon lime juice

2 garlic cloves

½ teaspoon salt

½ teaspoon ground cumin

½ teaspoon oregano

Pound the chicken until it is ½ inch thick, and cut it into 1-inch-wide strips. Place the chicken into a zip-top plastic bag along with the salsa, oil, lime juice, garlic cloves, salt, cumin, and oregano. Squeeze the excess air from the bag, seal it, then shake to mix and thoroughly coat the chicken.

Refrigerate 1 to 2 hours, turning the bag every 15 minutes.

Drain the chicken, saving the marinade. Thread the chicken onto skewers.

Place the chicken on the grill or broiler rack, and brush with the marinade. Grill 6 to 8 minutes, turning and basting with the marinade, until cooked through.

Serve with additional salsa.

Makes 6 to 8 servings.

Mustard Chicken

Mustard Marinade:

½ cup Dijon mustard

3 tablespoons olive oil

1 tablespoon crushed
   dried tarragon leaves

½ teaspoon freshly ground pepper

4 to 6 boneless, skinless
   chicken breast halves

Vegetable oil for brushing grill

TIP

This tangy grilled chicken is great in sandwiches for those folks who don't want a hamburger.

Prepare a charcoal grill or preheat a gas grill to high.

Prepare the Mustard Marinade by combining the mustard, olive oil, tarragon, and pepper in a bowl.

Pound the chicken breasts lightly between two pieces of plastic wrap. Place them in a shallow dish and pour the marinade over them. Turn a couple times to make sure they are well coated. Marinate the chicken at room temperature for 15 minutes to 1 hour.

Brush the grill grate with vegetable oil. Remove the chicken from the marinade and place it directly over the fire. Cover the grill and cook on one side about 4 minutes. Turn and cover again, and cook for an additional 4 minutes, or until the juices run clear when pierced with a fork.

Serve immediately.

Makes 4 to 6 servings.

Grilled Garlic-Lime Chicken

2½ pounds chicken pieces

2 tablespoons olive oil

1 tablespoon seasoned salt

1 teaspoon seasoned pepper

3 or 4 limes

1 tablespoon garlic salt

In large bowl toss the chicken with the oil, seasoned salt, and seasoned pepper. Place in a large zip-top plastic bag and keep cold until ready to grill.

Cut the limes into quarters and keep cold.

Preheat a grill to medium heat. Grill the chicken about 30 minutes, or until thoroughly cooked. Turn the chicken frequently, sprinkling lightly with garlic salt after each turn. While the chicken is cooking, squeeze the lime quarters over it.

Makes 8 to 10 servings.

TIP

Whenever possible, do any chopping, slicing, or cutting at home before you head to the stadium. You can easily transport your cut items in baggies in your cooler, and doing these tasks in advance saves you both time and trouble at the game.

Sauerkraut Brats

1 (12-ounce) can beer

¼ cup water

1 medium onion, chopped loosely, divided

1 package bratwurst

1 (14.4-ounce) can sauerkraut

2 teaspoons brown sugar (or more to taste)

Bacon (1 strip per brat)

Combine the beer and water in a medium-size pot and bring the liquid to a boil. Add half the chopped onion and the brats and boil them for 5 minutes.

While the brats are boiling, combine the sauerkraut, the remaining chopped onion, and the brown sugar in a pan. If there is not much liquid from the sauerkraut, add a little bit of water. Bring to a boil and continue cooking until the liquid is reduced almost completely and the sugar has caramelized.

Remove the brats from the pot, slice them down the middle, and stuff them with some of the sauerkraut. Wrap one piece of bacon around each brat and secure it with toothpicks.

Place the brats on the grill and cook until browned and crispy on the outside, turning occasionally.

Serve on a kaiser bun with the condiments of your choice.

Makes 8 servings.

Grilled Beef Kebabs and Vegetables

Asian Marinade:

1²/₃ cups red wine vinegar

1¼ cups ketchup

¾ cup olive oil

¾ cup soy sauce

½ cup teriyaki sauce

2 tablespoons mustard

1 tablespoon salt

1 tablespoon pepper

1 tablespoon garlic-pepper seasoning

2 pounds beef tenderloin, cubed

4 bell peppers, quartered

4 white onions, cut into chunks

1 (16-ounce) package whole
  fresh mushrooms

4 tomatoes, quartered

To make the Asian Marinade, mix the vinegar, ketchup, oil, soy sauce, teriyaki sauce, mustard, salt, pepper, and garlic-pepper together in a shallow dish. Add the tenderloin, bell peppers, and onions. Cover the dish and place in the refrigerator for 6 to 8 hours or overnight.

Add the mushrooms and the tomatoes and place again in the refrigerator until ready to cook.

On metal grill skewers, alternately place one piece of beef, onion, bell pepper, mushroom, and tomato.

Place the skewers on the grill and cook slowly over low heat, basting with the remaining sauce while cooking.

Place the skewers on a platter to serve.

Makes 4 to 5 servings.

Play-Action Burgers

2 pounds ground beef

2 tablespoons mesquite seasoning

1 (8-ounce) package cheese slices

1 large onion, thinly sliced

2 tomatoes, thinly sliced

Salt

Pepper

Mix the ground beef with the mesquite seasoning and shape into eight patties—thinner, but larger, than usual. On top of four of the patties place a layer of cheese, sliced onion, and sliced tomato. Cover with the remaining patties and seal the edges. Season to taste with the salt and pepper.

Grill over low heat until done (probably a little longer than usual or about 20 to 25 minutes), turning regularly.

Makes 4 servings.

Variety Is the Spice of Burgers

1 pound lean ground beef or turkey
(use 1¼ pounds meat for
milder flavor)

1 packet spices and seasonings

Combine the meat with the seasoning packet of choice (see options below). Mix thoroughly and shape into patties.

Grill the patties for 7 to 10 minutes, turning once.

Top with your choice of garnishes and serve.

Makes 4 burgers.

Chili Burgers:

1 (1.25-ounce) packet chili seasoning
Top the burgers with your choice of
grilled onions, cheddar cheese, lettuce,
and tomato.

Fajita Burgers:

1 (1.25-ounce) packet fajita seasoning
Top the burgers with your choice of
grilled onions and salsa, and consider
serving on onion buns rather than plain
hamburger buns.

Taco Burgers:

1 (1.25-ounce) packet taco seasoning
Top the burgers with your choice of
guacamole, salsa, jalapeño Jack cheese,
lettuce, and tomato.

Italian Burgers:

1 (1.25-ounce) packet
spaghetti sauce spices
Top the burgers with your choice of
Mozzarella cheese, Romaine lettuce, and
mayonnaise mixed with garlic powder.

Steak and Mushroom Sandwich

1 pound beef round tip steak
  or sirloin tip steak, thinly sliced

Salt and pepper

½ plus ½ teaspoon dried thyme

1 tablespoon olive or vegetable oil

2 cloves garlic, minced

½ pound sliced white mushrooms

¼ cup dry red wine

½ cup prepared beef gravy

½ loaf French bread, split
  and toasted

Sprinkle the meat with the salt and pepper to taste and ½ teaspoon thyme. Sauté the meat (using half the oil) until browned and medium rare, about 30 to 45 seconds per side. Cook the meat in batches and do not overcrowd the pan— this will ensure that the meat fries rather than steams.

In a large nonstick skillet heat the remaining oil over medium-high heat. Add the garlic and cook for 1 minute. Add the mushrooms and cook, stirring until tender, about 3 to 5 minutes. Pour in the wine and bring to a boil for 1 minute. Season the mushrooms with salt and pepper to taste and the remaining ½ teaspoon thyme. Add the prepared gravy and stir until the mixture is heated.

Arrange the meat on top of the toasted French bread and top it with the mushroom sauce.

Makes 4 to 6 servings.

Barbecued Ribs

10 pounds pork or beef ribs

Salt

Pepper

Garlic powder

Creole seasoning

1 cup Worcestershire sauce

1 (12-ounce) can 7-Up or beer

Favorite barbecue sauce

Wood chips of your choice
(hickory or pecan are
good options)

On the day before cooking, place the ribs in a deep aluminum tray. Season to taste with salt, pepper, garlic powder, and Creole seasoning. Add the Worcestershire sauce to the tray. Add enough 7-Up or beer to almost cover the ribs. Cover and refrigerate overnight.

On game day light the fire and allow it to die down a bit. Move the coals to one end of the grill, and then place the ribs on the opposite end. Shut the lid of the grill and allow the ribs to cook 4 to 6 hours. During cooking, turn the ribs several times and baste with the barbecue sauce. This will seal in the flavor. Wood chips can be added to the fire anytime during cooking.

Makes 12 to 15 servings.

TIP

Always brush your grill grate with oil to help keep your food from sticking.

White Bean Chili

2 tablespoons vegetable oil

1 onion, chopped

2 cloves garlic, minced

1 (14.5-ounce) can chicken broth

1 (18.75-ounce) can tomatillos,
   drained and chopped

1 (16-ounce) can diced tomatoes

1 (7-ounce) can diced green chiles

½ teaspoon dried oregano

½ teaspoon ground coriander seed

¼ teaspoon ground cumin

Kernels from 2 ears fresh corn

1 pound chicken meat,
   cooked and diced

1 (15-ounce) can white beans

Salt

Ground black pepper

Optional Toppings:

Limes (for squeezing)

Cilantro

Tortilla chips

Avocado

Cheese

Heat the oil in a large pot and cook the onion and garlic until soft.

Stir in the broth, tomatillos, tomatoes, chiles, oregano, coriander, and cumin. Bring to a boil and simmer for 10 minutes.

Add the corn, chicken, and beans. Simmer for 5 minutes. Season with the salt and pepper to taste. Squeeze a slice of lime over top if desired.

Serve with a selection of toppings.

Makes 8 servings.

Surprise Chili

1 tablespoon olive oil

1 pound lean ground beef

1½ cups chopped onion

2 cloves garlic, chopped

1 (28-ounce) can crushed tomatoes

1 (14.4-ounce) can sauerkraut

1 (15-ounce) can pinto beans

1 (14-ounce) can beef broth

3 to 4 tablespoons chili powder

¼ teaspoon pepper

Heat the oil in a large saucepan over medium heat. When hot, add the ground beef, onions, and garlic. Cook until browned. Drain the fat. Stir in the tomatoes, sauerkraut, pinto beans, beef broth, chili powder, and pepper, and bring to a boil. Reduce the heat to low and then simmer, partially covered, for 25 to 30 minutes.

Makes 4 to 6 servings.

Grilled Fish Kebabs

2 red bell peppers

1 medium zucchini

1 pound swordfish

1 pound salmon

24 cherry tomatoes

1 cup lightly packed fresh basil

½ cup olive oil

1 garlic clove

Salt

Pepper

eat the grill to high.

Cut the red bell peppers and the zucchini into bite sized pieces. Cut the swordfish and salmon into twenty-four 1½-inch cubes and thread—against the grain—onto eight skewers, alternating the fish with a cherry tomato, a piece of red bell pepper, and a piece of zucchini.

In a blender purée the basil, olive oil, and garlic until smooth. Season the purée with salt and pepper to taste. Reserve half of the mixture.

Brush the kebabs with half of the basil mixture and season them with salt and pepper.

Place on the grill and cook until the fish is opaque, 6 to 10 minutes, turning occasionally.

With a clean basting brush, coat the kebabs with the reserved basil mixture and serve.

Makes 4 servings.

Steel City Afterburner Breakfast

2 pounds Italian sausage

2 large onions, chopped

2 (14-ounce) cans
sliced potatoes

1 dozen eggs

1 (12-ounce) jar salsa

2 dozen large tortillas

1 (16-ounce) package
shredded Mexican cheese

Brown the sausage in a large pot. (This can be done at home the day before, but if you do cook it ahead make sure to save the grease to cook with the next morning).

Remove the sausage from the pot and sauté the onions and potatoes in the grease.

Return the sausage to the pot and add in the eggs and salsa. Turn the heat down to low and cook, stirring constantly, until the eggs are done to your liking.

Heat the tortillas. Place a spoonful of the sausage mixture onto a tortilla and sprinkle with cheese.

Roll up, tucking in the ends of the tortilla, and serve.

Makes 18 to 24 servings.

Frogmore Stew

5 quarts water

¼ cup Old Bay seasoning
   plus additional for serving

4 pounds small red potatoes

2 pounds kielbasa or
   hot smoked link sausage,
   cut into 1½-inch pieces

6 ears fresh corn, halved

4 pounds unpeeled, large
   fresh shrimp

Cocktail sauce

Bring the water and Old Bay seasoning to a rolling boil in a large covered stockpot.

Add the potatoes. Return to a boil and cook, uncovered, for 10 minutes. Add the sausage and corn, and return to a boil. Cook for 10 minutes or until the potatoes are tender.

Add the shrimp to the stockpot. Cook for 3 to 4 minutes or until the shrimp turn pink. Drain the contents of the pot, and pour the stew into a large serving bowl.

Serve with Old Bay seasoning and cocktail sauce.

Makes 12 servings.

Herbed Beer Bread

Shortening or cooking spray

3 tablespoons cornmeal

4 cups self-rising flour

3 tablespoons sugar

½ cup Parmesan cheese

1 tablespoon dried Italian herbs

12 ounces beer at room temperature

2 tablespoons soft butter
   or margarine

Preheat the oven to 325°.

Grease a loaf pan with shortening or cooking spray, and sprinkle the bottom and sides with the cornmeal.

In a large bowl combine the flour, sugar, cheese, and dried herbs. Mix well. Gradually stir in the beer to make a stiff batter. Pour the batter into the pan.

Bake for 50 minutes. Brush the loaf with the softened butter. Turn the loaf out of the pan and let it cool on a wire rack.

Makes 1 loaf.

Soft Pretzels

Preheat the oven to 450°

Stir the sugar into ¼ cup warm water in a small bowl. Sprinkle the yeast over the top. Let stand for 10 minutes. Stir to dissolve the yeast.

Combine the remaining 1½ cups warm water with the flour and salt in a large bowl. Stir the yeast into the mixture. Add a bit more flour, if needed, so the dough isn't too sticky.

1 teaspoon sugar

1½ plus ¼ cups warm water, divided

1¼ teaspoons active dry yeast

4½ cups all-purpose flour

½ teaspoon salt

1 egg white

1 teaspoon water

2 tablespoons kosher salt

1 tablespoon sesame seeds

Knead the dough for 8 to 10 minutes, until it is smooth and elastic. Place the dough in a greased bowl, turning once to grease the top. Cover with a tea towel and let the dough stand in the oven with the light on and the door closed for about 45 minutes, or until doubled in bulk.

Remove the dough from the oven and punch it down. Roll the dough into a log. Mark the dough into twelve portions and cut. Roll each portion into a ½-inch rope. Shape each rope into a pretzel form on greased baking sheets. Beat the egg white and the 1 teaspoon water with a fork in a small bowl. Brush this egg glaze onto the pretzels. Sprinkle some of the pretzels with kosher salt and some with sesame seeds.

Bake for about 15 minutes. Turn out onto racks to cool.

Makes 12 pretzels.

Crispy Snack Mix

2 cups corn and rice cereal

1 cup tiny pretzel twists

½ cup small wheat crackers

½ cup cheddar crackers

1½ tablespoons melted butter

1 tablespoon ginger stir-fry sauce

1 teaspoon chili powder

1 teaspoon ground cumin

¼ teaspoon salt

Cooking spray

Preheat the oven to 250°.

Combine the corn and rice cereal, pretzels, wheat crackers, and cheddar crackers in a large bowl. Combine the butter, stir-fry sauce, chili powder, cumin, and salt. Drizzle this mixture over the cereal and crackers in the bowl. Toss to coat. Coat a jelly-roll pan with cooking spray. Spread the cereal mixture evenly into the jelly-roll pan.

Bake for 30 minutes, or until crisp, stirring twice.

Makes 4 cups.

Mango Salsa 🏠

1 mango, peeled, seeded, and chopped (about 1½ cups)

1 medium sweet red pepper, seeded and finely chopped

¼ cup thinly sliced green onions

1 Scotch bonnet or hot green chile pepper, finely chopped and seeded

3 tablespoons olive oil

½ teaspoon finely grated lime peel

2 tablespoons lime juice

1 tablespoon vinegar

¼ teaspoon salt

¼ teaspoon ground black pepper

In a medium bowl stir together the mango, sweet red pepper, green onions, chile pepper, oil, lime peel, lime juice, vinegar, salt, and black pepper.

Store in the refrigerator up to 24 hours.

Makes 2 cups.

Green Goddess Dip

1 cup mayonnaise

2 cups sour cream

$\frac{1}{4}$ cup minced fresh chives

2 garlic cloves, minced

$\frac{1}{3}$ cup minced, fresh parsley leaves

2 tablespoons tarragon vinegar

1 tablespoon freshly squeezed lemon juice

3 anchovy fillets, minced

$\frac{1}{2}$ teaspoon sea salt

$\frac{1}{4}$ teaspoon finely ground black pepper

Place the mayonnaise, sour cream, chives, garlic, parsley, vinegar, lemon juice, anchovies, sea salt, and black pepper in a food processor fitted with a steel blade. Pulse about 12 times to mix, scrape down the sides of the bowl, and then pulse another 6 to 8 times.

Transfer the mixture to a serving bowl. Press plastic wrap against the surface of the dip to prevent a skin from forming and refrigerate.

This dip is best after being chilled 6 to 8 hours or overnight.

Makes 2 cups.

Beer Cheese Spread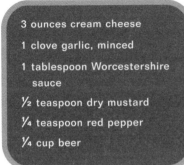

3 ounces cream cheese

1 clove garlic, minced

1 tablespoon Worcestershire sauce

½ teaspoon dry mustard

¼ teaspoon red pepper

¼ cup beer

In a large mixing bowl beat the cream cheese until very smooth. Add the garlic, Worcestershire sauce, mustard, and red pepper, beating well to combine completely. Gradually add the beer and beat until well blended.

Chill for one hour before serving.

Makes 1 cup.

Uno! Dos! Tres! Fiesta Bean Spread 🏠

1 (16-ounce) can refried beans

1 cup salsa

1 teaspoon ground cumin

½ teaspoon garlic powder

1 pint sour cream

1 (1.25-ounce) package taco seasoning mix

2 cups shredded cheddar cheese

1 cup shredded Monterey Jack cheese

1 bunch green onions, chopped

2 tomatoes, chopped

Bottom layer: Mix together the beans, salsa, cumin, and garlic powder. Spread into a large, flat serving dish as a thin layer, maybe ½ inch thick.

Middle layer: Mix together the sour cream and taco seasoning. Spread this mixture over the bean layer.

Top layer: Combine the cheddar and Monterey Jack cheeses and sprinkle them on top of the sour cream layer. Last, sprinkle the green onions and tomatoes over all.

Cover with plastic wrap and chill for about an hour.

Serve cold with tortilla chips.

Makes 24 to 30 servings.

Asparagus and Sugar Snap Peas with Dipping Sauce 🏠

Place 2 to 3 cups cold water in a large stockpot and bring to a rapid boil. Add the asparagus and blanch for 2 minutes. Add the peas and blanch for an additional 1 minute. Remove the vegetables from the stove, drain, and fill the pot with cold water to stop the vegetables from cooking further. Let the vegetables sit in the cold water for 5 minutes, and then drain and pat them dry with paper towels. Once the asparagus and snap peas have cooled, place them in large zip-top plastic bags and store them in your refrigerator.

1/2 pound asparagus, trimmed

1/2 pound sugar snap peas, trimmed

Honey-Mustard Dip:

3 tablespoons Dijon mustard

1/4 cup lemon juice

1/4 cup honey

3 tablespoons white wine vinegar

3 tablespoons finely chopped fresh dill

1/4 cup extra virgin olive oil

1/2 teaspoon salt

1/4 teaspoon pepper

For the Honey-Mustard Dip, in a medium-size mixing bowl add the mustard, lemon juice, honey, vinegar, and dill. Slowly whisk in the olive oil. Add the salt and pepper and stir. Cover and put the dip into the refrigerator for 30 minutes to chill.

When you are ready to serve the vegetables at your tailgate, place the asparagus and snap peas on a plate and remove the cover from the dip container. Place the dip near the vegetables to serve.

Makes 6 servings.

Grilled Portobello Mushrooms with Blue Cheese

8 portobello mushrooms,
about 4 inches in diameter

½ cup vegetable oil

Chopped fresh herbs of your
choice (suggestions: thyme,
basil, oregano, or chives)

⅓ to ½ cup crumbled
blue cheese

Remove the stems from the mushrooms and, if desired, scoop out the gills with a small spoon to make more room for the cheese. Clean the mushrooms and lightly brush both sides with the oil.

Place the mushrooms cap side down on the grill. Cook over medium-high heat 2 to 3 minutes. Turn the caps over, sprinkle with the herbs and cheese to taste, and cook 2 to 3 minutes more, or until the mushrooms are tender and the cheese has partially melted.

Serve warm.

Makes 8 servings.

Beer-Battered Fried Vegetables 🏠

2²/₃ cups all-purpose flour

2 cups beer

2²/₃ cups vegetable oil for frying

3 eggs

1¹/₃ cups milk

Salt

Pepper

1½ large carrots, cut into
  thick strips

1½ onions, sliced into rings

10 fresh mushrooms, stems removed

1½ green bell peppers, sliced
  into rings

In a medium bowl mix together 2 cups flour and the beer with a wooden spoon. Let the mixture stand for at least 3 hours at room temperature.

Heat the oil to 375°.

Mix the eggs and milk in a small bowl. In a separate bowl mix together the ²/₃ cup flour and the salt and pepper to taste.

Dip the carrots, onions, mushrooms, and peppers in the egg and milk mixture. Next dip the vegetables into the flour and seasoning mixture. Finally dip the vegetables in the beer and flour mixture. Place the vegetables into the oil and fry until golden brown.

Makes 8 servings.

Kickin' Corn on the Cob

6 fresh ears of corn

Chili Butter:

4 tablespoons unsalted butter

½ teaspoon chili powder

Dash of cayenne pepper

¼ teaspoon kosher salt

2 tablespoons minced
   fresh cilantro

Prepare a hot fire in a charcoal grill or preheat a gas or electric grill to high.

Pull back the husk to expose each ear of corn, but do not remove it. Remove the silk and then recover the corn with the husk. Run water into the ears of corn, drain the excess, and twist the husks at the top to close.

Prepare the Chili Butter by combining the butter, chili powder, cayenne pepper, kosher salt, and cilantro in a small bowl.

Place the corn directly over the hot fire. Grill for about 20 minutes, turning several times during cooking to get all sides. Remove from the grill and pull back the husks. You can either discard them or knot them at the base of the corn.

Brush the ears generously with the Chili Butter. Serve hot.

Makes 6 servings.

Corn Pudding

4 eggs

2 teaspoons salt

1 teaspoon pepper

1 teaspoon nutmeg

2 tablespoons grated onion

4 tablespoons butter

4 cups milk

4 cups cooked corn

Preheat the oven to 325°.

Grease a 9 x 13-inch casserole dish.

In a large bowl add the eggs, salt, pepper, nutmeg, and onion and beat well.

In a saucepan over moderate heat melt the butter. Stir in the milk and heat until warm. Fold the butter and milk mixture into the egg mixture and then stir in the corn

Pour the corn and egg mixture into a greased casserole dish.

Bake for 1 hour, remove from the oven, and let cool.

Before leaving for the tailgate, reheat the pudding and pour it into a thermal container to keep warm. When ready to serve at the tailgate site, serve from the container.

Makes 8 servings.

Summery Squash

2 tablespoons vegetable oil

1 small onion, sliced

2 medium tomatoes, coarsely chopped

1 teaspoon salt

¼ teaspoon pepper

2 small zucchini, cut into ½-inch slices

2 small yellow summer squash, cut into ½-inch slices

1 bay leaf

½ teaspoon dried basil

Heat the oil in a large skillet over medium heat. Cook and stir the onion about 5 minutes, until tender. Mix in the tomatoes and season with the salt and pepper. Continue to cook and stir about 5 minutes. Mix in the zucchini, yellow squash, bay leaf, and basil. Cover, reduce the heat to low, and simmer 20 minutes, stirring occasionally. Remove the bay leaf before serving.

Makes 6 servings.

Blackberry Spinach Salad

3³/₄ cups rinsed and dried
  baby spinach

2½ cups fresh blackberries

½ pound feta cheese, crumbled

2½ cups halved cherry tomatoes

1¼ green onions, sliced

¼ cup plus 1 tablespoon finely
  chopped walnuts (optional)

Balsamic vinaigrette dressing
  (optional)

Combine the spinach, blackberries, cheese, tomatoes, onions, and walnuts (if using) in a large bowl. Drizzle the dressing over the top, if you like.

Makes 6 servings.

Dilly Beans

1 pound trimmed green beans

1 to 2 cloves garlic, minced

10 or more sprigs fresh dill

1 teaspoon red pepper flakes

½ teaspoon dill seeds

½ teaspoon mustard seeds

Cider Vinegar Marinade:

1 cup cider vinegar

1 cup water

3 tablespoons sugar

½ teaspoon salt

Steam the beans over boiling water for 7 minutes, or until tender-crisp. Rinse immediately in cold water, and then place the beans into a glass or ceramic bowl. Add the garlic, dill, red pepper, dill seeds, and mustard seeds.

For the Cider Vinegar Marinade combine the vinegar, water, sugar, and salt in a saucepan, and bring the mixture to a boil. Pour over the beans, let cool, and cover.

Refrigerate for at least 10 hours. Serve cold.

Makes 8 servings.

Sesame Noodle Salad 🏠

1 pound spaghetti

8 ounces snow peas, slivered lengthwise

1 red bell pepper, cut into strips

½ cup smooth peanut butter

2 garlic cloves

1 jalapeño pepper, seeds removed

¼ cup soy sauce

¼ cup rice vinegar

⅓ cup warm water

2 tablespoons toasted sesame oil

¼ teaspoon salt

In a large pot of boiling, salted water, cook the spaghetti until al dente, according to the package directions. Drain and rinse with cold water.

In a large bowl combine the pasta with the snow peas and red bell pepper.

In a blender purée the peanut butter, garlic cloves, jalapeño pepper, soy sauce, rice vinegar, water, sesame oil, and salt.

Pour the dressing over the noodles and toss to coat. Serve chilled or at room temperature.

Makes 4 servings.

Oktoberfest Potato Salad 🏠

3½ pounds peeled and sliced potatoes

½ cup plus 1 tablespoon chopped onion

½ cup plus 1 tablespoon mayonnaise

¼ cup plus 2 teaspoons vegetable oil

½ cup plus 1 tablespoon cider vinegar

2 tablespoons plus ¾ teaspoon white sugar

2 tablespoons plus ¾ teaspoon dried parsley

2¼ teaspoons salt

Ground black pepper

Bring a large pot of salted water to a boil. Add the potatoes and cook them until tender but still firm, about 15 minutes. Drain the potatoes and transfer them to a large bowl. Add the onions.

In a separate large bowl whisk together the mayonnaise, oil, vinegar, sugar, parsley, salt, and pepper to taste. Gently stir in the potatoes and onion.

Let stand for 1 hour before serving to enhance the flavors.

Makes 8 servings.

Antipasto Salad

1 (10-ounce) package salad greens (about 10 cups)

1 (6-ounce) can pitted ripe olives, drained and halved

10 pepperoncini peppers

8 slices hard salami, quartered

1 cup shredded Mozzarella cheese

³/₄ cup Italian dressing

Place the greens, olives, peppers, salami, cheese, and dressing in a large bowl. Toss and serve.

Makes 4 servings.

Spiced Peaches

½ cup brown sugar

½ cup cider vinegar

6 whole cloves

3 whole allspice

1 (2½-inch) cinnamon stick

2 pounds fresh peaches, cut in half, pits removed, or 2 (16-ounce) cans peach halves

In a large saucepan combine the sugar, vinegar, cloves, allspice, and cinnamon stick. Bring to a boil and simmer 5 minutes. If using fresh peaches, just add them to the saucepan. If using canned peaches, drain them and add to the saucepan. Cook for 5 minutes more.

Remove from the heat and allow the peaches to cool. They can be served warm or cold.

Fix the peaches before leaving for the game. If you want to serve them warm, place the peaches in a thermal container.

However, if you prefer them cold, allow the peaches to cool for at least 1 hour. Place them in a plastic container and seal tight. Place in an ice chest.

Makes 7 to 8 servings.

Bread Pudding with Amaretto Sauce 🏠

1 (10-ounce) loaf stale French bread, crumbled (or 6 to 8 cups any type bread)

2 cups heavy cream

2 cups Amaretto

2 cups sugar

8 teaspoons melted butter

3 eggs

2 teaspoons vanilla

3 cups toasted slivered almonds

1 teaspoon cinnamon

1 teaspoon nutmeg

Amaretto Sauce (recipe follows)

Combine the bread, cream, Amaretto, sugar, butter, eggs, vanilla, almonds, cinnamon, and nutmeg. The mixture should be very moist, but not soupy. Pour into a buttered 9 x 12-inch (or larger) baking dish.

Place the dish in a cool (not preheated) oven. Turn the oven to 350° and bake for approximately 1 hour and 15 minutes, or until the top is golden brown.

Serve warm topped with the warm Amaretto Sauce.

Makes 16 to 20 servings.

Amaretto Sauce

8 teaspoons butter

1½ cups confectioners' sugar

2 egg yolks

½ cup Amaretto (or to taste)

In a medium-size saucepan cream the butter and sugar over medium heat until all the butter is absorbed. Remove from the heat and blend in the egg yolks. Gradually pour in the Amaretto, stirring constantly. Serve warm over the warm bread pudding. The sauce will thicken as it cools.

Peanut Butter Swirl Brownies 🏠

Adjust the oven rack to the middle position and preheat the oven to 350°.

Line an 8-inch baking dish with foil, making sure to leave some foil hanging over the edges of the dish. Coat the foil with cooking spray.

Melt the chocolate and butter in a small bowl in the microwave or in a heatproof bowl set over a pan of simmering water. Stir the mixture occasionally to combine. Once melted, let the mixture cool for several minutes.

Whisk the sugar, baking soda, salt, eggs, and vanilla together in a medium bowl until combined, about 15 seconds. Whisk in the chocolate mixture until smooth. Stir in the flour until no streaks of flour remain. Scrape the batter evenly into the prepared pan.

Drop the peanut butter in small dollops over the batter. Without touching the foil lining, run a paring knife through the batter to create swirls.

Bake until a toothpick inserted halfway between the edge and the center of the pan comes out clean, 22 to 27 minutes.

Cool the brownies on a wire rack until they are at room temperature, about 2 hours. Using the foil, lift the brownies from the pan to a cutting board. Slide the foil out from under the brownies, and cut the brownies into 2-inch squares.

Makes 16 brownies.

Cooking spray

3 ounces chopped, unsweetened chocolate

8 tablespoons unsalted butter, cut into chunks

1 cup sugar

$\frac{1}{2}$ teaspoon baking soda

$\frac{1}{4}$ teaspoon salt

2 large eggs

1 teaspoon vanilla extract

$\frac{2}{3}$ cup all-purpose flour

$\frac{1}{3}$ cup peanut butter at room temperature

Carrot Cupcakes 🏠

Paper muffin cups

1 cup sugar

⅓ cup vegetable oil

2 tablespoons orange juice

½ teaspoon vanilla extract

2 large eggs

1 teaspoon baking powder

½ teaspoon baking soda

½ teaspoon ground allspice

½ teaspoon salt

¾ cup plus 2 tablespoons flour

1½ cups shredded carrots

½ cup chopped walnuts

¼ cup shredded coconut,
plus extra for garnish

Cream Cheese Frosting
(recipe follows)

Preheat the oven to 350°.

Line standard muffin tins with the paper muffin cups.

In a bowl combine the sugar, oil, orange juice, vanilla extract, and eggs. Stir in the baking powder, baking soda, allspice, and salt. Add the flour and mix thoroughly. Stir in the carrots, walnuts, and coconut.

Distribute the batter evenly among twelve muffin cups, and bake until a toothpick inserted in the center comes out clean, about 25 minutes.

When the cupcakes have cooled, top each one with a spoonful of the Cream Cheese Frosting and garnish with the remaining coconut.

Makes 12 servings

Cream Cheese Frosting

8 ounces cream cheese,
room temperature

¾ cup confectioners' sugar

¼ teaspoon vanilla extract

Combine the cream cheese, confectioners' sugar, and vanilla in a small bowl and stir until well combined.

Chocolate Rum Cake

Preheat oven to 325°. Grease and flour a bundt pan. Combine the rum, cake mix, pudding mix, eggs, oil, and coffee. Beat at medium speed for 2 minutes and then stir in the chocolate chips and flaked coconut.

Spread evenly into the pan and bake for 1 hour. Cool in the pan for 15 minutes, remove from the pan, and cool completely.

Prick the top of the cake with a fork. Brush the Coffee Glaze all over the top and sides of the cake until the glaze is absorbed. Garnish with the coconut.

Makes 12 servings.

- $^3/_4$ cup coconut rum
- 1 package chocolate cake mix
- 1 package instant chocolate pudding mix
- 4 large eggs
- $^1/_2$ cup oil
- $^1/_2$ cup chocolate chips
- $^3/_4$ cup flaked coconut
- $^3/_4$ cup strong coffee
- Coffee Glaze (recipe follows)

Coffee Glaze

- $^1/_2$ cup powdered sugar
- 2 tablespoons coffee
- 4 tablespoons coconut rum

Combine the sugar, coffee, and rum in a small bowl.

DRINK INDEX

Nonalcoholic Drinks

Drinks

Bavarian Coffee

NONALCOHOLIC

6 ounces freshly brewed hazelnut-
   flavored coffee
2 tablespoons mocha/
   chocolate syrup
1 tablespoon maraschino cherry juice

Whipped cream
Shaved chocolate or miniature
   chocolate chips
Maraschino cherries

Combine the hot coffee, syrup, and cherry juice in a mug, mixing well. Top with whipped cream, chocolate shavings, and a cherry. Serve immediately.

Makes 1 serving.

Hot Spiced Cider

¼ cup light molasses
2 quarts cider
1 teaspoon whole allspice
1 teaspoon whole cloves

1 (3-inch) cinnamon stick
Dash of nutmeg
Pinch of coriander

Combine the molasses and cider. Tie the spices in cheesecloth and add to the cider mixture. Slowly bring to a boil. Cover and simmer 20 minutes. Remove the spices.

Makes 10 to 12 servings.

Laurie's Iced Tea

1 gallon water
4 family-size tea bags
1 handful fresh mint
 (about 6 to 7 sprigs)

2⅔ cups sugar
1½ cups orange juice
1 cup lemon juice
1 liter ginger ale

Boil the water, add the tea bags, and steep for 10 minutes. Remove the bags and add the mint and sugar. Stir to dissolve the sugar. Let the tea mixture cool. Add the orange juice and lemon juice and refrigerate until ready to serve. Just before serving, add the ginger ale. Best if served over crushed ice.

Makes 30 servings.

Mint Citrus Sparkler

1 quart tonic water
1 quart grapefruit juice
½ quart fresh orange juice
1 cup lemon juice

$\frac{1}{4}$ cup fresh-squeezed lime juice
Ice
1 lemon, thinly sliced
1 handful fresh mint leaves

NONALCOHOLIC

In a gallon pitcher or punch bowl, combine the tonic water, grapefruit juice, orange juice, lemon juice, and lime juice. Stir to combine. Add the ice and lemon slices. Bruise the mint leaves by "chopping" them with the back edge of a knife or tearing them slightly with your hands. Add the mint leaves to the sparkler mix and stir to mix through. Let stand 10 minutes.

Makes 20 servings.

Piña Colada Slush

2 cups cubed fresh pineapple
1½ cups pineapple juice, chilled
¼ cup cream of coconut

1 cup ice cubes
1 cup vanilla ice cream

Place the pineapple in the freezer and freeze one hour or until firm. Remove from the freezer and let stand 10 minutes. Combine the pineapple juice and cream of coconut in a blender. With the blender on, add the pineapple cubes and ice cubes ½ cup at a time, and process until smooth. Add the ice cream and process until smooth. Serve immediately.

Makes 6 to 8 servings.

Potion Punch

NONALCOHOLIC

3 (12-ounce) containers frozen
  apple juice
9 cups water

½ cup lime juice
½ gallon softened lime sherbet
9 cups chilled club soda

Prior to leaving for the stadium, combine the apple juice, water, and lime juice. Cover and chill. Just before serving, spoon the lime sherbet into a large punch bowl. Slowly pour the apple juice mixture and club soda over the top and stir gently.

To create a potion-like fog on top of the punch, add a small amount of dry ice directly to the bowl. Most grocery stores sell dry ice.

Makes 24 servings.

Apple Martini

½ cup vodka

¼ cup apple juice

¼ cup apple schnapps

Thin slices of Granny Smith
apples for garnish

Combine the vodka, apple juice, and apple schnapps in a shaker with ice. Shake really well so that the ice is broken into shards. Strain into two martini glasses and garnish each with a slice of apple.

Makes 2 servings.

Bloody Mary

1 quart V-8 juice

2 lemons, juiced and strained

2 tablespoons Worcestershire sauce

Tabasco sauce

Salt and pepper

1½ cups vodka

1 lime, juiced

Celery sticks (optional,
for garnish)

Lime wedges (optional,
for garnish)

Combine the V-8, lemon juice, Worcestershire, Tabasco to taste, salt and pepper to taste, and vodka in a pitcher. Squeeze the lime into the mix and garnish with the small lime wedges and celery, if using.

Makes 8 servings.

Blue Hawaiian

2 ounces light rum

2 ounces Blue Curaçao

4 ounces pineapple juice

2 ounces cream of coconut

2 cups ice

Cherries for garnish

Blend the rum, Curaçao, pineapple juice, cream of coconut, and ice in a blender at high speed. Pour into highball glasses and garnish with a cherry.

Makes 2 servings.

Conga Rita

2 ounces orange rum
2 ounces coconut rum
2 ounces pineapple rum

Margarita/sour mix
Lime wedges for garnish

Combine the orange, coconut, and pineapple rums in a glass. Add the margarita/sour mix and shake to combine. Serve on the rocks, or combine the ingredients in a blender with ice and blend until smooth. Serve garnished with a lime wedge.

Makes 2 servings.

Creamsicle

1¾ cups crushed ice
1½ cups cracked ice (or 6 cubes)
1 ounce orange vodka
½ ounce Tuaca

2 ounces half-and-half
1 teaspoon sugar
Splash of orange juice
Orange slice and vanilla bean
 for garnish

Fill a 12-ounce glass with the crushed ice. Fill a cocktail shaker with the cracked ice (or ice cubes), vodka, Tuaca, half-and-half, sugar, and orange juice. Shake vigorously to blend. Strain the mixture into the glass of crushed ice. Garnish the glass with the slice of orange and add the vanilla bean as a swizzle stick.

Makes 1 serving.

Frozen Gladiator

3 ounces tequila
4 ounces pineapple juice
2 tablespoons lime juice

2 cups crushed ice
Pineapple wedges for garnish

- -

Combine the tequila, pineapple juice, lime juice, and ice in a blender and blend at low speed. Pour into old-fashioned glasses and garnish with a pineapple wedge.

Makes 2 servings.

Gin and Sin

2 ounces gin
2 ounces lemon juice
2 ounces orange juice

Ice
Grenadine

Combine the gin, lemon juice, and orange juice in a cocktail shaker filled with ice. Add a couple of dashes of the grenadine. Shake well until the contents are chilled. Strain into martini glasses.

Makes 2 servings.

Hot Buttered Rum

4 ounces dark rum
1 tablespoon butter plus 1
   teaspoon for topping
1 teaspoon light brown sugar

Nutmeg
Powdered cloves
Boiling water
Cinnamon sticks

In a large mug combine the rum, 1 tablespoon butter, brown sugar, and a pinch each of the nutmeg and cloves. Add the boiling water to fill the mug, and stir the contents until the sugar has dissolved. Pour into two serving mugs. Garnish with a cinnamon stick and top with the remaining 1 teaspoon butter.

Makes 2 servings.

Key Lime Martini

3 ounces vanilla rum
Pineapple juice
Fresh lime juice

Midori
Ice

Mix the rum into a glass of pineapple juice. Add a splash of fresh lime juice and Midori. Add ice and shake well until chilled. Strain and pour into martini glasses.

Makes 2 servings.

Lemony Ginger Freeze

1 cup tequila

½ cup Triple Sec

Juice of 2 lemons

2 tablespoons freshly grated ginger

2 cups ice cubes

Lemon slices for garnish

Combine the tequila, Triple Sec, lemon juice, ginger, and ice cubes in a blender and blend to a smoothie-like consistency. Serve in glasses garnished with a slice or twist of lemon.

Makes 4 servings.

Luau Punch

2 cups dark rum
1 cup pineapple rum
2 cups strawberry purée or
   grenadine syrup
¼ cup fresh lime juice

3 cups pineapple juice
2 cups orange juice
½ cup Simple Syrup (page 156)
Ice cubes
Orange and lime slices for garnish

In a pitcher or a punch bowl combine the dark rum, pineapple rum, strawberry purée, lime juice, pineapple juice, orange juice, and Simple Syrup. Cover and chill until ready to serve. Just before serving add the ice cubes and float fresh orange and lime slices in the bowl.

Makes 24 servings.

Madras

1 ½ ounces vodka

4 ounces cranberry juice

1 ounce orange juice

Lime wedge for garnish

Pour the vodka, cranberry juice, and orange juice into a highball glass containing ice. Garnish with a wedge of lime.

Makes 1 serving.

Mexican Coffee

1 ounce coffee liqueur

½ ounce tequila

5 ounces very hot black coffee

Whipped cream

Stir the coffee liqueur and tequila together in a coffee cup. Add the coffee and top with the whipped cream.

Makes 1 serving.

Mint Julep

Mint leaves plus 1 sprig
  for garnish
2 ounces bourbon

Dash of Simple Syrup
  (recipe follows)

- -

Muddle the mint leaves with a muddler or the back of a spoon in the bottom of a cocktail glass. Add 1 ounce bourbon and fill the glass with crushed ice. Add the remaining ounce of bourbon and a dash of Simple Syrup. Garnish with a sprig of fresh mint.

Makes 1 serving.

- -

Simple Syrup

1 cup water

2 cups sugar

- -

Put the water and sugar in a small saucepan. Heat to a boil while stirring. Reduce the heat and continue to stir until the sugar dissolves. Cool to room temperature. Using a funnel, pour the liquid into a container that will hold at least 1½ cups. Seal and store in the refrigerator indefinitely. Use whenever a recipe calls for simple sugar or simple syrup.

Makes about 2 cups.

Vampire

Ice

4 ounces vanilla rum

Sprite or 7-Up

Grenadine

Fill two highball glasses with ice and add 2 ounces of vanilla rum to each. Fill with Sprite or 7-Up and top the drink off with a splash of grenadine.

Makes 2 servings.

Watermelon Limeade

8 cups chopped seedless
   watermelon (about 6 pounds)
½ cup fresh lime juice
   (about 4 limes)

2 tablespoons sugar
½ cup vodka
Mint for garnish (optional)

- -

Working in batches, purée the watermelon in a blender. Add the lime juice and sugar. Continue to purée until the mixture is smooth. Transfer the purée to a pitcher and add the vodka. Cover and chill until ready to serve. Garnish with mint if you desire.

Makes 2 quarts.

Zombie

1 ounce unsweetened pineapple juice

Juice of 1 lime

Juice of 1 small orange

1 teaspoon confectioners' sugar

½ ounce apricot brandy

2½ ounces light rum

1 ounce Jamaican rum

1 ounce passion fruit syrup
  (optional)

½ cup crushed ice

Red cherries for garnish

Green cherries for garnish

½ ounce 151-proof rum

Fresh mint for garnish

Put the pineapple juice, lime juice, orange juice, confectioners' sugar, brandy, light rum, Jamaican rum, syrup (optional), and ice into a blender, and blend at low speed for 1 minute. Strain the mixture into a chilled highball glass. Decorate with 1 red and 1 green cherry. Carefully float the 151-proof rum on top and add a sprig of mint. Serve with a straw.

Makes 2 servings.

Tailgater's Food Safety

If there are few things more delightful than creating a memorable tailgate party, then there is surely nothing more miserable than developing food or alcohol poisoning as a result of attending. Because we want you to be safe while having a really, seriously fun time, we've compiled the following advice for those who will be cooking and drinking far from the safety of their kitchens.

Follow these guidelines and you'll stand a better chance of living to tailgate another day.

FOOD

Be sure to thoroughly wash your hands before, during, and after preparing food for a tailgate party. Lather with soap and water for at least twenty seconds. If you don't want to bring lots of extra water with you to your tailgate, hand-sanitizing gel or antibacterial wipes are good alternatives.

Defrost meats in the refrigerator or in the microwave—not at the tailgate. Marinate meat in the refrigerator as well, and don't reuse the marinade unless it's been boiled.

Keep raw or thawed meat tightly sealed in a plastic bag or wrapped in plastic wrap for the trip to the tailgate. Consider packing meat products in one cooler and additional food in another, to prevent juices from contaminating other food items.

Raw meats and ready-to-eat foods should always be kept separate. Pack extra or color-coded plates and utensils to help prevent cross-contamination. Use one set for raw foods and the other for cooked foods.

Always cook foods to proper temperatures. A meat thermometer is the only reliable way to ensure foods are safe to eat. Hamburgers and bratwurst should be cooked to 160°F and chicken breasts to 170°F.

Use a well-insulated cooler with plenty of ice or icepacks to keep temperatures below 40°F for storing food. Keep a refrigerator thermometer inside the cooler to monitor the temperature.

Transport coolers in your trunk rather than in a heated car during cool weather—the cold temperatures outside will help keep food chilled. In warmer climates, do the opposite. Transport coolers in the backseat of your air-conditioned car rather than a hot trunk, especially for long road trips.

Carry-out and preprepared foods are also susceptible to contamination, so use the same care with them as with foods brought from home.

Throw away perishable food before heading into the stadium, unless you plan to keep it refrigerated at 40°F or below during game time. Food should not be left out for more than two hours. In hot weather (90°F or above) the safe time is reduced to one hour.

After the game, serve and eat only nonperishable foods unless you stored your pregame leftovers in a cooler so they remained at 40°F or below.

ALCOHOL

The following drinks contain equal amounts of alcohol and are often referred to as a drink or a standard drink:

• One 12-fluid-ounce bottle of beer or wine cooler
• One 5-fluid-ounce glass of wine
• One mixed drink containing 1.5 fluid ounces of 80-proof hard liquor, such as gin, whiskey, or rum

"Proof" is the amount of alcohol in hard liquor or distilled spirits. The percentage of pure alcohol in hard liquor is usually one-half the proof. For example, 100-proof liquor is about 50 percent pure alcohol. The higher the proof, the more alcohol the liquor contains.

Most people can metabolize one standard alcoholic drink per hour—that's one 12-ounce beer, one 5-ounce glass of wine, or one mixed drink.

If you're making drinks that use cream, half-and-half, or other spoilable products, keep those products in the cooler until they're needed, then put them back immediately. Don't let them sit out for easy access.

Always eat food when drinking and pace your drinks, to keep from getting too intoxicated.

WHEN TO CALL 911

Sometimes having too many drinks results in alcohol poisoning. When that happens, call a doctor instead of letting someone "sleep it off." Gently turn this person on his or her side to prevent choking after vomiting. Signs and symptoms of alcohol poisoning include

• Unconsciousness or semiconsciousness
• Slow breathing—eight breaths or less per minute, or lapses of more than eight seconds between breaths
• Cold, clammy, pale or bluish skin
• A strong odor of alcohol

We know we've tossed out a lot of tips, ideas, and ways to improve your parking-lot party. We've also told you about a lot of things you may want to pack in your car.

Now we're going to help you find all that stuff and start you on your journey to ultimate tailgtating.

First, there are a couple of things every tailgater should have before getting started.

One is a membership in the American Tailgaters Association. The ATA is a national organization that promotes tailgating, negotiates discounts on merchandise for members, and allows tailgaters to meet in forums, discuss the best tailgating places, talk about their favorite teams or sports, and post pictures. Basically, it's the one-stop tailgaters' "community." *The Ultimate Tailgater's Handbook* is the official tailgating handbook of the ATA. They have a few membership options, including the basic membership, which is free.
You can't beat that.

The other is a Screenserver. This is a new variety of screensaver . . . one that receives updated images, news, and information all day long. This new entertainment product displays a combination of magazine-quality photography, TV-quality video, and broadcast-quality audio, along with breaking news, statistics, and archives typically found on Web sites. And you can have it right on your desktop. Pretty cool. Actually, really cool and free.

Log on to www.theultimatetailgater.com to see if your favorite team has a Screenserver yet and download it. Be sure to check back often because the folks who create them are adding new teams all the time.

In the following pages, you'll find information and shopping resources for the tailgating topics discussed in this book. In the Venue Guide (beginning on page 172), you'll find complete tailgating guides for more than 175 venues across America.

GRILLS

There's just all kinds of stuff out there on the Web about grills. Type in "buy a grill" on Google and you'll get thousands of listings. Below are the company sites for the larger grill manufacturers. This is a good place to start, since these sites will have the most details on the specs and styles of grills available.

www.webergrills.com
www.ducane.com
www.hollandgrill.com
www.thebrinkmancorp.com
www.campchef.com

Now, if what you want is something custom-made and really big, check out www.bbqpits.com. This company from Houston can set you up right.

And remember, you can also check your local hardware stores, Wal-Mart, or Lowe's. In fact, www.lowes.com has a feature that allows you to compare grills so you can find the one just right for you.

GRILL ACCESSORIES

You'll need tools for cooking on and cleaning off your grill and a fine selection of those items can be found at the sites listed below.

www.cooking.com
www.campingworld.com
www.grillingaccessories.com
www.lowes.com

Want even your food to be loyal to the team? At www.thegrillstoreandmore.com, you'll find university-specific branding irons for your steaks . . . an awfully nice touch.

GENERATORS

Before you invest in a portable generator, you'll want to carefully pick the one that's right for your tailgating plans. Go to www.electric-generator-guide.com for basic information about selecting and purchasing a generator. The site has links that take you to places where you can purchase products online.

You can also check out www.generation-power.com for more information and ideas or go to www.theultimatetailgater.com to download our generator comparison chart.

TENTS

You can find canopy tents at sporting goods stores, your local Home Depot or Lowe's, or Wal-Mart. You might like shopping for tents at these stores because they usually have one or two samples set up, allowing you to get a sense of just how many people you could fit under them.

However, if armchair shopping is your preference, you can check out the Web sites below to do a little research and shopping. You'll also find more of a selection online than in a local store.

www.elitedeals.com
www.kdkanopy.com
www.championcanopies.com
www.ezupdirect.com

And if you want to add a historical element to your tailgate, the people at www.tentsmiths.com will sell you replicas of Viking tents, World War II officer's tents, teepees, and all sorts of other nifty things. These items are perfect to help you complete your theme tailgate. You'll be the only one in the parking lot with one, and the envy of all.

PARTY DECORATIONS

Basic party decorations can be found almost anywhere. Visit your local grocery store, Wal-Mart, Target, or a local party supply shop. If you prefer to do your shopping online, the sites below are good sources for basic decorations, and each one also has sections that can help you get set up for any of the theme tailgates.

www.4funparties.com
www.party411.com
www.partysupplyhut.com
www.partysuppliesandfavors.com
www.bulkpartysupplies.com

FOOD

When you want to add some authentic ethnicity to your buffet, you can order food, spices, and condiments from the nice folks at www.ethnicgrocer.com.

DECORATIONS OR INFORMATION FOR SPECIFIC THEMES

Luau Theme
www.hilohattie.com
www.islandmadness.com

Fiesta Theme
www.mariachi4U.com
www.partypop.com/categories/mariachi_bands.html

The team specific piñatas we mentioned can be found at www.pinatas.com.

Oktoberfest Theme
www.partyoptions.net/octoberfest/octoberfest_decorations.htm
www.germanfoods.org/consumer/oktoberfestexperience.cfm

Halloween Theme

There are some great pumpkin-carving patterns along with instructions on how to make patterns of your own at www.jack-o-lantern.com.

Of course, almost all cities have stores that sell costumes, props, and other Halloween gear, but if you want to order online and have these shipped to you, a good place to start is www.halloweenmagazine.com. Here you'll find costumes and music, and you can even catch up on what's new with Elvira (remember her?).

THE BAR

Your best bet for barware and accessories is going to be plastic (they don't easily break) and cheap (they will get lost). A number of stores from chains like Crate and Barrel and Pier 1 to local grocery stores and Wal-Mart will have plenty to choose from.

For team-specific drinkware and bar items, try the sites listed in the General Tailgating listing below.

For the ultimate tailgater who wants to take a full bar along to the game, you may want to visit www.ajmadison.com/cgi-bin/ajmadison/3BCSSS.html. It's really expensive, but really cool. (You can also find it at other retailers.)

GENERAL TAILGATING FUN

There are a number of tailgating supply sites on the Internet. The ones below have some of the widest selections, and you'll be able to find everything from tables and coolers to blenders and banners.

www.tailgatetown.com
www.americantailgater.com
www.mytailgate.com
www.footballfanatics.com

www.tailgatingsupplies.com
www.tailgatepartyshop.com
www.tailgated.com

DRESS THE PART

Finding the right clothing really shouldn't be too hard for you. Local team gear will show up in lots of stores around town as soon as the season starts. Plus a wide selection can be found at

www.footballfanatics.com
www.collegegear.com
www.teamstore.com
www.MVP.com

Additionally, each team's Web site will almost certainly have a link to a page where you can buy logo merchandise. Most of your local sporting goods stores will sell it, too. The sporting goods stores are more likely to sell merchandise for their hometown team, so you might have a slightly harder time finding Steelers gear in Atlanta. But like they say, where there's a die-hard fan looking to get dressed, there's a way.

PORTABLE TOILET

If you are one of the few who want to pack your potty for the parking lot, just type www.toilets.com into your Web browser and you can find the perfect portable toilet for you.

VENUE GUIDE: How to Use This Section

This section includes all NCAA Division I-A, NFL, and NASCAR venues in the United States. Each venue displays icons describing what you'll find, along with contact information and notes on each location. As of print time, all entries were correct. However, things can change. When in doubt, call the contact numbers listed to be sure the information you need is still current. Below is a key to what each icon means.

Remember—if you don't see an icon listed, that activity is forbidden entirely, restricted in some way, or doesn't apply to that location. Read the entry and call for further clarification, if necessary.

Decorations are allowed, excluding banners and signs that are advertising services or goods.

Alcohol is permitted for those of legal drinking age.

Grills or cookers are permitted for noncommercial use only.

Parking is more than $50 per day for cars or larger vehicles.

Parking is between $30 and $50 per day for cars or larger vehicles.

Parking is no more than $30 per day for any vehicle.

RVs may park overnight before or after the game.

Number of hours you can tailgate before game. Times exceeding 4 hours are included in "4" icon.

Number of hours you may remain after the event. Usually this includes tailgating, but read the entry to be sure.

RVs, limos, and other oversized vehicles are allowed.

Tents may be erected.

Tables, chairs, and other tailgating furniture are allowed.

Venue offers visible security presence in parking and tailgating areas.

Venue offers at least one paved parking lot.

Shuttle service available from parking or tailgating areas to the event and back again.

ACC CONFERENCE

CLEMSON UNIVERSITY

Clemson Memorial Stadium
Clemson, South Carolina
(864) 656-2118
1-800-CLEMSON

RVs can arrive Friday evening and park overnight if you call ahead, but not on campus. General parking opens at 7 a.m. Saturday. For those staying the weekend, Clemson's YMCA has parking spaces for little or no money. Shuttle to game from YMCA provided for little or no charge.

DUKE UNIVERSITY

Wallace Wade Stadium
Durham, North Carolina
(919) 684-8111 or (919) 668-4112

University offers affordable parking, good security, and relaxed attitude. In town for a long weekend? Bring your bike and hit the American Tobacco Trail or the Little River Regional Park & Nature Area for exercise and great scenery.

FLORIDA STATE UNIVERSITY

Doak Campbell Stadium
Tallahassee, Florida
(850) 487-1691 Tallahassee Civic Center

Stadium parking reserved for Boosters and donors. Best bet: park at Tallahassee Civic Center. Overnight parking $35; for two nights $60; no hookups; call ahead for permit. Shuttle from civic center runs 2 hours before until 1 hour after game, $3 round trip, under 12 years free.

GEORGIA INSTITUTE OF TECHNOLOGY

Bobby Dodd Stadium
Atlanta, Georgia
(404) 984-2000/parking extension
(404) 984-9645

RVs can drop anchor at Tech Parkway at 5 p.m. Friday. Display your parking pass to reach parking area smoothly. No parking on sidewalks, lawns, green space, or landscaped areas. Those who do will be "booted." For extended visits, Atlanta offers attractions such as botanical gardens, Six Flags Over Atlanta, the Georgia Aquarium, and even a skydiving school.

UNIVERSITY OF MARYLAND

Byrd Stadium
College Park, Maryland
(800) 462-8377

University prohibits kegs and grilling inside garages. Alcohol patrols, along with campus police, keep things under control. Keep everything orderly and you won't have any trouble.

UNIVERSITY OF MIAMI

Miami Orange Bowl
Coral Gables, Florida
(305) 284-6699

Tailgating here can be tricky: restrictions change from game to game. Parking around stadium for donors. Depending on location, prices range from $5 to $450. Call ahead for details and locations of available satellite lots. Shuttles available. Visit beach and tour Miami's Art Deco District.

NORTH CAROLINA STATE UNIVERSITY

Carter Finley Stadium
Raleigh, North Carolina
(919) 865-1500

Plenty of paramedics and police on call during game days. For medical emergencies, dial 911 and on-site ambulance will respond. Otherwise, relax and enjoy local tailgating treat— whole smoked or barbecued pig. Mmmm, good!

UNIVERSITY OF NORTH CAROLINA

Kenan Memorial Stadium
Chapel Hill, North Carolina
(919) 843-2000

RVs park in designated off-campus satellite lot at 5 p.m. day before game; you can start tailgating then. Expect to see lots of barbecue. Keep any alcohol in cups; no open containers allowed. Athletic department sponsors "Tarheel Town" with concessions and games for children. Worth a visit.

UNIVERSITY OF VIRGINIA

Scott Stadium
Charlottesville, Virginia
(800) 626-8723

Fontaine Research Park lots, free on first-come, first-served basis. Parking garage available, but not for tailgating. Numerous private lots around town. Those in university lots must use gas grills, not charcoal. Leave tents at home. Ham 'n' biscuits, fried chicken are local tailgate favorites.

Virginia Polytechnic Institute

Lane Stadium/Worsham Field
Blacksburg, Virginia
(540) 231-6000

Donors park in designated lots close to stadium. Some public parking lots exist on campus, but very few. Tents aren't allowed; tailgaters are limited to one space. Alcohol permitted only in donor lots. This rule is not strictly enforced, as long as nondonors are discreet. Most people park in different lots throughout town—shuttles offered to and from stadium.

Wake Forest University

Groves Stadium
Winston-Salem, North Carolina
(336) 758-5753

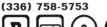

Buses, RVs, and other large vehicles park in LJVM Coliseum across Deacon Blvd., or at city-run campground across street with RV connections available. No gas-powered generators, glass containers, or external stereo systems allowed. Keep drinks in cans or cups only; keep tents in grassy areas. On the other hand, kegs are permissible.

BIG EAST CONFERENCE

Boston College

Alumni Stadium
Boston, Massachusetts
(617) 552-3000

Only donors allowed to park on campus. Visitors park off campus free in university-rented lots. Most are a good distance away—shuttles provided. Tailgating pretty much reserved for donors, alumni. No tailgating in off-campus lots. On the bright side, you're in Boston; visit Faneuil Hall Marketplace or Boston Harbor Islands.

University of Connecticut

Renschler Field
Storrs, Connecticut
(877) 288-2666

Gates open 8 a.m. game day for all vehicles. Keep tailgate coolers or grills in front of, or behind, cars. No kegs, no large or charcoal grills, no glass, no tossing footballs or Frisbees, no blocking traffic.

UNIVERSITY OF PITTSBURGH

Heinz Field
Pittsburgh, Pennsylvania
(412) 648-8200

Parking lots open first thing in the morning, tailgating begins then. Keep alcohol in cups; erecting tents is prohibited. Policies can change; call ahead.

RUTGERS UNIVERSITY

Rutgers Stadium
New Brunswick, Piscataway, New Jersey
(732) 445-2766 ticket office
(732) 445-4223 facilities

Parking lots open 3 hours before kickoff; only 15-minute walk to stadium. No kegs allowed; no open fires. Hanging opposing-team mascot in effigy is perfectly fine. Tailgaters can stay until sundown.

SYRACUSE UNIVERSITY

Carrier Dome
Syracuse, New York
(315) 443-2121 ticket office
(315) 443-4652 parking

RVs can park 6 p.m. day before game and stay overnight at Sky Top Road lot. Call -4652 number to reserve space. Keep fires safely contained. Out-of-towners will love two local tailgate specialties: Hoffman hot dogs, salt-potatoes.

TEMPLE UNIVERSITY

Lincoln Financial Field
Philadelphia, Pennsylvania
(215) 204-6267

University and stadium are in downtown Philadelphia, so parking is decentralized. Most parking within walking distance. If parked across town, shuttles and public transportation available. Never had authentic hoagie or Philly cheesesteak sandwich? Now's your chance!

WEST VIRGINIA UNIVERSITY

Mountaineer Field
Morgantown, West Virginia
(304) 293-3541 ticket office
(304) 293-5621 athletic dir.

Handy tip: park at coliseum for free and take shuttle to game; otherwise you pay $40 for RV parking. Call ahead for RV permit. Leave kegs and artificial noisemakers at home.

::::::::::::::::::::::::::::::::::::

BIG TEN CONFERENCE

::::::::::::::::::::::::::::::::::::

UNIVERSITY OF ILLINOIS

Memorial Stadium
Urbana-Champaign, Illinois
(217) 333-3631

Lots open at 7 a.m. Visitors should arrive at stadium from south or east for easier parking. No pole tents, no ground fires, pop-up tents okay. Security checks for underage drinkers. Depart by 11 p.m.

INDIANA UNIVERSITY

Memorial Stadium
Bloomington, Indiana
(812) 855-4848 parking ext.
(812) 855-4822 Alumni Assoc.

RVs can arrive night before, parking in "purple lot." Others park 8 a.m. game day. No tents, large tarps, couches, big indoor or outdoor furniture, or large sound systems. Small canopies are okay; keep beverages in plastic cups. Cars leave by midnight; RVs may stay overnight. Complete information at http://iuhoosiers.com/football/gameday.html.

UNIVERSITY OF IOWA

Kinnick Stadium
Iowa City, Iowa
(319) 335-9411

Gates open at 7 a.m. Beer and wine allowed; no kegs or hard liquor. Keep drinks in cups. Stay within your space; leave when ready. Don't miss Rally Alley and food vendors on Melrose Ave.

UNIVERSITY OF MICHIGAN

Michigan Stadium
Ann Arbor, Michigan
(734) 647-BLUE

RVs park at Pioneer High School's Purple Lot, southwest corner of Main St. and Stadium Blvd. Cost for RV parking $105. Lot available for RVs 5 p.m. day before game, ending noon next day. No advance reservations made: first-come, first-served.

MICHIGAN STATE UNIVERSITY

Spartan Stadium
East Lansing, Michigan
(517) 355-1855

Tailgate next to vehicle or in grassy areas nearby, starting 5 hours before game. Be aware of general traffic patterns. Leave drinking game paraphernalia at home. One lot reserved as alcohol-free. Catch band as they march through tailgating area.

UNIVERSITY OF MINNESOTA AT MORRIS

Hubert H. Humphrey Metrodome
Minneapolis, Minnesota
(612) 625-4879

University shares Metrodome with Minnesota Vikings; overnight parking isn't practical. Tailgating restricted to main Metrodome lot, some Washington Ave. lots. Tailgating starts 3 hours before game. Open fires not allowed.

NORTHWESTERN UNIVERSITY

Ryan Field
Evanston, Illinois
(847) 491-7887

Good news—overnight RV parking $30. Bad news—all must leave 2 hours after game. No real restrictions; just keep within own tailgate space. Wildcat Alley has fun games for younger kids.

OHIO STATE UNIVERSITY

Ohio Stadium
Columbus, Ohio
(800) 462-8257

RVs can park in lots along Fred Taylor Drive. Gates open 7 a.m.; all spots are within walking distance. No open containers of alcohol. Most tailgaters leave 2 or 3 hours after game.

PENNSYLVANIA STATE UNIVERSITY

Beaver Stadium
State College, Pennsylvania
(814) 863-3489

Penn State's overnight RV lots available for $50 per night, two nights prior to game day. Call ahead for same-day pass—prices can be cut in half! No open fires, charcoal grills, or fireworks. Some lots allow tents, others don't; call ahead to find out.

PURDUE UNIVERSITY

Ross-Ade Stadium
West Lafayette, Indiana
(800) 497-7878

RVs park in special lots day of game. Visitors can park overnight in reserved club-member spots, but must leave by 7 a.m. for club members. Don't hog space; no alcohol in parking lots adjacent to high school or armory.

UNIVERSITY OF WISCONSIN

Camp Randall Stadium
Madison, Wisconsin
(608) 262-8683

Call ahead for updated parking availability, especially buses, RVs, other oversized vehicles. No overnight parking. Shuttles available for distant lots. Check for updates: www.uwbadgers.com/facilities/index.aspx.

::::::::::::::::::::::::::::::::::::

BIG TWELVE CONFERENCE

::::::::::::::::::::::::::::::::::::

BAYLOR UNIVERSITY

Floyd Casey Stadium
Waco, Texas
(254) 710-8183

Oversized vehicles park overnight at track stadium $20. Cars park in Tailgate

Alley $5. No alcohol allowed on campus or in Touchdown Alley. Alcohol served at George's Bar, in a 40 x 40-foot tent across street, off campus. Strict security; space-saving discouraged. Touchdown Alley has food vendors, live music; free to general public.

UNIVERSITY OF COLORADO

Folsom Field
Boulder, Colorado
(303) 492-1411 parking ext.

Tailgaters park in fields or lots; farthest is ½ mile from stadium. Parking $20 for cars, up to $80 for oversized vehicles. No overnight parking, oversized cookers in fields, charcoal grills, or open containers of alcohol. Free shuttle into city of Boulder.

IOWA STATE UNIVERSITY

Jack Trice Stadium
Ames, Iowa
(515) 294-5022

Only donors use parking lots next to stadium; visitors use grass lots across street, first-come, first-served. No kegs allowed; bring drinks in cans, not bottles. RVs can spend the night after game, but can't park a day in advance.

UNIVERSITY OF KANSAS

Memorial Stadium
Lawrence, Kansas
(785) 864-3946

Parking begins morning of game, tailgating 3 hours before game. Call for updated parking prices. Shuttles available for distant lots. No tailgating once game begins. No set departure time, but those tailgating after game can be ticketed.

KANSAS STATE UNIVERSITY

KSU Stadium
Manhattan, Kansas
(800) 221-2287

No parking overnight before or after game. Tailgating and parking start 5 hours before game. No real restrictions except tailgaters must stay within own space.

UNIVERSITY OF MISSOURI—COLUMBIA

Memorial Stadium
Columbia, Missouri
(573) 882-5195

Stadium parking for donors only; visitors park off campus. Public RV lots grant two spaces to park, two more to tailgate; cost is $50 for weekend. No real restrictions on tailgating items; use common sense. Game-day tents are set up around campus with food, bands.

UNIVERSITY OF NEBRASKA

Memorial Stadium
Lincoln, Nebraska
(402) 472-1960

RVs park night before game; money collected next morning. Tailgating starts 3 hours before game. Stay within your space; no kegs or open fires allowed.

UNIVERSITY OF OKLAHOMA

Oklahoma Memorial Stadium
Norman, Oklahoma
(800) 522-0772 ext. 2345
(405) 325-3311
(405) 325-4666 RV information

RVs park at Lloyd Noble Center 1½ miles from campus. Spaces with electric hookups $40; no hookups only $15. Tailgating begins on arrival. Shuttle runs 2 hours before and after game, $3 each way. No kegs or open fires allowed.

OKLAHOMA STATE UNIVERSITY

Boone Pickens Stadium
Stillwater, Oklahoma
(405) 744-5737

Free public RV parking lot on campus, 1 mile west of stadium! Park night before and walk 200 yards to shuttle. All campus public parking very limited. Most parking reserved for club members. Instead, private lots rent to visitors. Keep alcohol in cups; stay within your space. Leave morning after game.

UNIVERSITY OF TEXAS

Darrell K Royal—Texas Memorial
Stadium
Austin, Texas
(800) 982-2386 ticket office
(512) 471-4441 UT police

Lots surrounding stadium reserved for Longhorn Foundation members. Tailgating for nonmembers, visitors can be difficult. Visitor parking $10; RVs stay free in lot ½ mile from campus on east side of I-35, starting 5 p.m. night before game. Unclear if season pass is needed; call ahead.

TEXAS A&M UNIVERSITY

Kyle Field
College Station, Texas
(979) 862-PARK

Two nearby RV parks offer parking, $35 daily, minimum two-night stay for games. Campus parking opens 7 a.m. game day. Parking passes required: $2 per hour, $12 per day. Call ahead or go to www.transport.tamu.edu for parking. Try the smoked beef brisket!

TEXAS TECH UNIVERSITY

Jones SBC Stadium
Lubbock, Texas
(806) 742-4260

RVs can park night before, across from stadium. Parking free around stadium. No restrictions other than staying within your space. They've got brisket, too!

CONFERENCE USA

UNIVERSITY OF ALABAMA AT BIRMINGHAM

Legion Field
Birmingham, Alabama
(205) 975-8224

Bad news—RVs not allowed in campus lots. Good news—cars $5 a space; extra spaces can be purchased. Arrive early to beat traffic; stay within your space(s).

UNIVERSITY OF CINCINNATI

Nippert Stadium
Cincinnati, Ohio
(513) 556-2287
www.ucbearcats.com

Two lots for RVs, first-come, first-served. All parking within walking distance. Stay within space; no charcoal grills; must have fire extinguisher; alcohol in cups only. Important: call ahead; tailgating info may change due to campus construction.

EASTERN CAROLINA UNIVERSITY

Dowdy-Ficklen Stadium
Greenville, North Carolina
(252) 328-4500
(252) 328-4503

Call ahead for RV parking; spaces may be available after 5 p.m. Friday. Contact -4503 to make arrangements. Parking limited on campus. RVs must be self-contained; no electrical hookups available. No kegs; tents allowed for own space only; keep alcohol in cups; stay within your space. After game, Atlantic coast only an hour away.

UNIVERSITY OF HOUSTON

Robertson Stadium
Houston, Texas
(713) 743-GOUH

Visitors park in Blue Lot on campus, $5 for cars. RVs park overnight in separate area, must get special parking pass $100–$200. Be prepared for hot weather; bring sunscreen.

UNIVERSITY OF LOUISVILLE

Papa John's Cardinal Stadium
Louisville, Kentucky
(502) 852-5863

Most visitors park at fairgrounds. Long walk from stadium, but only $5. RVs park at Kentucky Fair and Exposition Center—preferred entry at Gates 1 and 6. However, information may change—call ahead.

UNIVERSITY OF MEMPHIS

Liberty Bowl Memorial Stadium
Memphis, Tennessee
(901) 729-4344

RVs can park a day in advance; all parking within walking distance of stadium. May purchase extra spaces if needed. No tailgating in handicapped spaces. Don't miss city's excellent attractions, including children's museum and zoo.

UNIVERSITY OF SOUTH FLORIDA

Raymond James Stadium
Tampa, Florida
(800) 462-8557

Parking available game day only, including RVs. All parking within walking distance. Tents not recommended. Visit International Plaza while in town.

UNIVERSITY OF SOUTHERN MISSISSIPPI

M. M. Roberts Stadium
Hattiesburg, Mississippi
(601) 266-5299 Eagle Club

Parking fills up fast; many stake out spots night before. No special place for RVs; there's parking on Hillcrest St., but it's a long walk. Keep alcohol concealed. Parking is free!

TEXAS CHRISTIAN UNIVERSITY

Amon G. Carter Stadium
Fort Worth, Texas
(817) 257-5658

RVs park night before game (Friday) on campus RV lot; $50 for weekend.

Parking, tailgating spots vary in distance; shuttles provided for distant lots. No open fires; alcohol must be concealed.

Tulane University

Louisiana Superdome
New Orleans, Louisiana
(504) 861-WAVE
(504) 587-3633 Superdome

Tailgating done on top floor of parking garage and on concourse area of Superdome. All grills rented from Superdome, $25. Try gumbo, 'gator, boudin sausages; visit French Quarter down the street. Come hungry, have fun—everybody's friendly!

U.S. Military Academy at Westpoint (Army)

Michie Stadium
West Point, New York
(845) 446-0538

Good news—free parking. Bad news—close spots only for season ticket holders. Shuttles are available. Tailgating starts 8 a.m. game day. No weapons or hazardous items. Security very strict; all vehicles searched. Hey, at least you're safe.

INDEPENDENT

University of Notre Dame

Notre Dame Stadium
South Bend, Indiana
574-631-7356

Range of parking prices (cars $15–$35 depending on lot, to $45 for RVs) makes Notre Dame affordable. No overnight parking available; RVs restricted to one lot. No tailgating during game; no tents, charcoal grills, or kegs; stay within your space.

UNITED STATES NAVAL ACADEMY (NAVY)

Navy-Marine Memorial Stadium
Annapolis, Maryland
(800) 874-6289 ticket office

Stadium parking sold season pass first, then single game passes. Parking sold on first-come, first-served basis, but not on game day. All passes bought in advance. RVs only $20. No overnight parking, saving spaces, or fireworks. Shuttles available from downtown. Make time to explore Annapolis.

MID-AMERICAN CONFERENCE

UNIVERSITY OF AKRON

Rubber Bowl
Akron, Ohio
(888) 99-AKRON

Tailgating done in grassy area; no overnight parking, but affordable. Keep alcohol in plastic cups. Kids' activities at stadium; food tents are open.

BALL STATE UNIVERSITY

Ball State Stadium
Muncie, Indiana
(765) 285-1474

Lots next to stadium for donors only; grass lots for non-season ticket holders; tailgating lot on Bethel Road. Alcohol not allowed on campus. Bring lawn furniture; grill your heart out. Leave tent, banners home. Legal drinkers use discretion. Parking is cheap.

BOWLING GREEN STATE UNIVERSITY

Doyt L. Perry Stadium
Bowling Green, OH
(806) 742-4260

Separate lots for donors and visitors. Tailgate Park, adjacent to stadium, sells hospitality tents for $200–$1,000 to groups. Visitors park on campus for $5, RVs for $10. RVs can arrive a day or two early.

UNIVERSITY AT BUFFALO

University Stadium
Buffalo, New York
(716) 645-3177

All parking within walking distance; no parking overnight. Keep alcohol in cups; leave keg or beer ball at home.

UNIVERSITY OF CENTRAL FLORIDA

Florida Citrus Bowl
Orlando, Florida
(407) 823-4653

Parking within walking distance. RV lots are just outside stadium; go to www.clickandpark.com for specifics.

Call ahead to get tickets for game. No overnight parking or kegs; grill yourself silly; bring sunscreen and drink fluids.

CENTRAL MICHIGAN UNIVERSITY

Kelly/Shorts Stadium
Mount Pleasant, Michigan
(888) FIRE-UP-2

RVs owners call ahead for overnight permit or game-day parking. Tailgate next to your vehicle. Families can purchase tailgating packages from university—get table, chairs, etc.; set up in grassy area near pond. No pull-behind grills, kegs, or glass bottles. Tents used in designated areas only. Tailgating ends when game begins.

EASTERN MICHIGAN UNIVERSITY

Rynearson Stadium
Ypsilanti, Michigan
(734) 487-2282

Parking is free; leave glass containers and kegs home. Leave by nightfall. Not many people tailgate here, so plenty of room for you.

KENT STATE UNIVERSITY

Dix Stadium
Kent, Ohio
(330) 672-3350

Stadium is off campus; parking surrounds stadium. Parking available on campus, with shuttle to game. No overnight parking; gates open 6 hours before game. University personnel say no restrictions on tailgating items. University Web site says tailgating lot opens 1 p.m., with no alcohol allowed. Don't say we didn't warn you.

MARSHALL UNIVERSITY

Joan C. Edwards Stadium
Huntington, West Virginia
(800) 843-4373

Visitors park off campus. Two blocks west of campus is parking garage for $10, or park on street. RVs have special lot requiring a donation; call for prices. No overnight parking. Keep inside your space; no kegs; don't tailgate inside parking garage. No, really, someone tried.

MIAMI UNIVERSITY

Yager Stadium
Oxford, Ohio
(513) 529-1620

Up to 4 hours before game, parking is free; afterwards cars pay $7, RVs pay $14. RVs park in RV City. No overnight parking; no alcohol allowed.

NORTHERN ILLINOIS UNIVERSITY

Huskie Stadium
DeKalb, Illinois
(815) 753-1923

Must obtain permit to have tent.
There's no overnight parking. All
parking within walking distance.

OHIO UNIVERSITY

Peden Stadium
Athens, Ohio
(740) 597-1358 (740) 593-4491
(740) 597-1375

Most tailgating done in Pepsi Tailgate
Park grass lot. Alcohol allowed only there;
can't buy extra spaces. RVs must park in
cement lots, but can buy extra spaces.
Don't park the night before; you'll be
towed. Tents not allowed; alcohol requires
permit; leave at end of game. Wise to call
ahead for information; try -1375 number.

UNIVERSITY OF TOLEDO

Glass Bowl
Toledo, Ohio
(419) 530-3611

Tailgating done in two specified lots; call
for location. Lax enforcement of no
alcohol rule—be discreet. No glass
bottles or overnight parking.

WESTERN MICHIGAN UNIVERSITY

Waldo Stadium
Kalamazoo, Michigan
(269) 387-8092

All parking $5; RVs have specified
lots; no overnight parking. All within
walking distance, but shuttles
available. No glass containers, kegs,
or couches; one space per vehicle.
Tailgating stops when game begins.

::::::::::::::::::::::::::::::::::

MOUNTAIN WEST CONFERENCE

::::::::::::::::::::::::::::::::::

BRIGHAM YOUNG UNIVERSITY

LaVell Edwards Stadium
Provo, Utah
(801) 422-2028

Parking surrounds most of stadium, all
free. RVs can park overnight for weekend
games, not on weekdays. Most fans leave
2 hours after game; RVs can spend night.
No alcohol, tobacco, or open fires. Dispose
of coals safely. BYU fans use Dutch ovens
on grills or coals for great dishes. Local
fans are very friendly—enjoy it.

COLORADO STATE UNIVERSITY

Hughes Stadium
Fort Collins, Colorado
(970) 491-6020

All parking outside stadium in huge unpaved lot. Visiting RVs have section just for them, but not overnight. A few lots reserved for large parties (50 people); visiting-team fans have own tailgating area—call ahead to arrange. Use plastic cups for drinks; use canopies, not spiked tents; keep it nice and calm.

UNIVERSITY OF LAS VEGAS

Sam Boyd Stadium
Las Vegas, Nevada
(702) 895-1533

RVs park free, but not overnight and not on grass. For $60 you can prereserve six grass spaces; otherwise one space costs $5. Kegs are okay; no glass bottles, grills, or open pit fires. Game times may change due to weather or ESPN schedule.

UNIVERSITY OF NEW MEXICO

University Stadium
Albuquerque, New Mexico
(505) 925-LOBO

RV parking available in any open lot except Tailgate 2 lot. Park within the lines. All parking free; donors get parking priority. Visitors park in lots around campus. No overnight parking; no glass containers, party balls, or kegs; no commercial tailgating. No tailgaters in parking lots after game begins. Must pack up 30 minutes after game ends.

SAN DIEGO STATE UNIVERSITY

Qualcomm Stadium
San Diego, California
(619) 283-7378

Qualcomm Stadium off campus, located on Friars Road. Parking surrounds stadium. Parking free before 1 p.m.; after that it's $7. No alcohol allowed. Tailgating very family oriented; visit Fun Zone for children's activities, live music, live radio show.

UNITED STATES AIR FORCE ACADEMY

Falcon Stadium
Colorado Springs, Colorado
(719) 472-1895
(719) 333-9021 events management

Parking's free, but no overnight parking. Large parties call events management; space very limited. No tailgating items restricted. Check online for parking maps at www.airforcesports.com.

University of Utah
Rice-Eccles Stadium
Salt Lake City, Utah
(801) 581-8849

Visitors park in various lots; season ticket holders use official tailgate lot. All within walking distance. Get your tailgate pass with your ticket. Overnight parking is available except for Thursday games. Alcohol's forbidden.

University of Wyoming
War Memorial Stadium
Laramie, Wyoming
(307) 766-4850

One huge official lot for tailgating—Tailgate Park. Park anywhere; alcohol allowed only in Tailgate Park. Parking in Tailgate Park reserved for donors. But no worries—everyone allowed in for free; it's a festival atmosphere with huge vendor tents, food for sale, etc. RVs have specific parking lots.

PACIFIC–10 CONFERENCE

University of Arizona
Arizona Stadium
Tucson, Arizona
(520) 621-CATS

RVs park on north side of campus in grass lot. Cost varies according to RV size. All spaces within walking distance. No overnight parking, kegs, or hard liquor. Campus provides some pregame activities.

Arizona State University
Sun Devil Stadium
Tempe, Arizona
480-965-2381

Visiting RVs park in Lot 4 across the street. Tailgating is done alongside vehicles. Tailgaters must stay within parking space. No tailgating within closed areas; no glass bottles. Don't save spaces; it's first-come, first-served.

University of California—Berkeley
Memorial Stadium
Berkeley, California
(800) GO-BEARS
(888) CAL-ALUM

No RV lots for visitors. Parking starts 7 a.m. game day; can be free or up to $50. Parking limited; many just go to Fun Zone hosted by school. Don't grill inside parking garage. No security in lots; lock up vehicle.

UNIVERSITY OF CALIFORNIA— LOS ANGELES

Rose Bowl
Los Angeles, California
(310) 825-5292

Parking starts 6 a.m.; no overnight parking. RVs have own lots; parking on first-come, first-served basis, starting 7 a.m. Tents larger than 10 x 10 feet need city permit; keep propane tanks away from brush. Area H is only place outside stadium to buy food.

UNIVERSITY OF OREGON

Autzen Stadium
Eugene, Oregon
(541) 346-4461

All visitors park across street from stadium. Tailgate next to vehicle or walk to donors' lot and join their party. Stay within parking space. Visit indoor practice facility; there's live music, food, and drink.

OREGON STATE UNIVERSITY

Reser Stadium
Corvalis, Oregon
(800) GO-BEAVS

Visitors park in paid lots around campus. RV visitors pay for two spaces to fit RV. Parking overnight allowed. Parking available at fairgrounds, a 10-minute walk; no shuttle.

UNIVERSITY OF SOUTHERN CALIFORNIA

Los Angeles Memorial Coliseum
Los Angeles, California
(213) 740-3843

Park at stadium or on campus. Ten-minute walk from campus to Coliseum. RVs can park at Coliseum, but not overnight. No real restrictions; security checks entering stadium take a long time.

STANFORD UNIVERSITY

Stanford Stadium
Stanford, California
(650) 723-1949 operations

Most stadium parking for donors, season ticket holders. There are some public lots. No spaces for visiting RVs; park in Stanford Shopping Center, walk to stadium. Most parking lots are free; some charge fees. One space per vehicle. Dirt lots: discarded coals must be buried in ground.

UNIVERSITY OF WASHINGTON

Husky Stadium
Seattle, Washington
(206) 543-2210

RVs park in E1 lot, starting Friday night. No alcohol (adults use discretion). "Sterngating": up to 5,000 people in Lake Washington tailgate on boats. Now that's fun!

WASHINGTON STATE UNIVERSITY

Martin Stadium
Pullman, Washington
(509) 335-8633
(509) 335-9684

RVs park in designated areas after 5 p.m. Thursday before game. No hookups, however. No tents, tables, or chairs in parking spaces or on sidewalks.

Some academic departments host parties on game days. Alcohol prohibited (adults use discretion). Hollingberry Fieldhouse hosts food fair 3 hours before and 90 minutes after game.

SOUTHEASTERN CONFERENCE

UNIVERSITY OF ALABAMA

Bryant Denny Stadium
Tuscaloosa, Alabama
(205) 348-6084
(205) 348-8391 parking services

Stadium parking for donors. Visitors (including RVs) park on campus wherever they find a legal spot. RVs can park on campus end of day Friday. Some lots charge fees; others don't. Tailgating starts on arrival. Tents with spikes are iffy at best; no other items forbidden. Please behave nicely.

UNIVERSITY OF ARKANSAS

Donald W. Reynolds Razorback Stadium & War Memorial Stadium
Fayetteville, Arkansas
(479) 443-9000
(479) 575-2000 Razorback Club
www.hogparking.com

All campus parking for donors. Visitors park free at Baum Baseball Stadium and are shuttled to game. RVs park overnight if you call -9000 number ahead of time. Some homeowners sell yard spots, $10 or $20. Keep alcohol use discreet; no grills in parking garages. Parking limited; come early.

AUBURN UNIVERSITY

Jordan-Hare Stadium
Auburn, Alabama
gameday@auburn.edu
www.ocm.auburn.edu/gameday

Visiting RVs park in designated lots. Parking free unless you're in private lot. Prices vary. RVs can arrive Friday 4 p.m.; must leave by 4 p.m. Sunday. Keep grills 50 feet from buildings. Barbecue and drinks served on Haley Concourse. Full guidelines on Web site.

UNIVERSITY OF FLORIDA

Ben Hill Griffin Stadium (The Swamp)
Gainesville, Florida
(352) 375-4683
(352) 392-8048
(352) 334-2600 RTS
www.gatorzone.com

Visitor RV parking first-come, first-served, starting 6 p.m. Friday, at Park and Ride lot next to Hilton Hotel and Conference Center off 34th Street. RVs must be gone by Sunday. No parking on sidewalks or grass; no alcohol. Shuttles available; contact RTS or go to www.go-rts.com for information. It's hot—drink plenty of fluids.

UNIVERSITY OF GEORGIA

Sanford Stadium
Athens, Georgia
(706) 542-2768
(706) 357-9613 Prestige Parking
www.prestigeparkingathens.com

Parking tight for all vehicles due to construction. Visiting RVs must call Prestige Parking for parking permit, location. Cars, go to Web site above for info. Prices not available at press time.

UNIVERSITY OF KENTUCKY

Commonwealth Stadium
Lexington, Kentucky
(859) 257-8000

General parking is north of Cooper Street. All lots surrounding stadium and south of Cooper are reserved for season ticket holders. Visitor RV lot opens 6 p.m. Friday, 1 mile from stadium; shuttle available. Stay within parking space; no alcohol, golf carts, or scooters. Commercial-sized grills need approval from athletic department. Security patrols stadium lots only. Leave 8 a.m. Sunday.

Louisiana State University

Tiger Stadium
Baton Rouge, Louisiana
(225) 578-8001
(225) 769-7805 Farr Park
www.lsusports.com

Visiting RVs park at Farr Park and take shuttle to game. All other RV parking for season ticket holders. Campus parking opens to visitors at 4:30 p.m. Friday. RVs can park Friday 8 a.m. in designated lots. The following are prohibited: commercial-sized grills, portable generators, alcohol, tents larger than 10 x 10 feet, open fires, motorbikes, four-wheelers, glass containers. Tents don't go under oak trees.

University of Mississippi

Vaught-Hemingway Stadium
Oxford, Mississippi
(662) 915-7522
(662) 915-7254 parking

There are two lots for RVs, one for season ticket holders; $600 with hookups, one without hookups free. Some RVers arrive as early as Wednesday, stay the weekend. No propane grills; no alcohol (keep in cup, be discreet); no parking on highway. Parking's tight; arrive early.

Mississippi State University

Davis Wade Stadium
Starkville, Mississippi
(662) 325-8121 special events
(662) 325-9114 game-day info
(662) 325-2600 ticket office
(662) 325-4140 facilities use

Visiting RVs assigned to two lots, can park Friday at noon. All must be gone by 7 a.m. Monday. Tailgating done in general picnic area. Small tents fine; don't dump charcoal on grass. Detailed info at http://msuinfo.ur.msstate.edu/parking/rules.html.

University of South Carolina

Williams-Brice Stadium
Columbia, South Carolina
(803) 777-4202

Visiting RVs park at State Fair Association at noon Friday, less than a mile away, and stay overnight. It has hookups. Stay within your space; no commercial-sized grills; don't block traffic. Note: some public parking lots do not have restrooms.

UNIVERSITY OF TENNESSEE
Neyland Stadium
Knoxville, Tennessee
(865) 974-1214
Bud Ford, Sports Info Director

No RV parking on main campus without permit. RVs park at Civic Coliseum and Blackstock Street lot behind Foundry at North World's Fair area. General parking also available at Civic Coliseum Parking Garage. Spaces available on a first-come, first-served basis. Shuttles available $4 each way. No alcohol, open fires, or tents. More info at http://utsports .collegesports.com/sports/m-footbl/ spec-rel/090204aaf.html.

VANDERBILT UNIVERSITY
Vanderbilt Stadium
Nashville, Tennessee
(615) 342-8525
www.commodoregameday.com
www.vucommodores.com

All parking is very close to stadium. Visiting RVs and buses park off campus in Harris-Hillman School parking lot on Blakemore (lots 106, 107, 108) beginning 5 p.m. Friday, leaving Sunday. No glass bottles, kegs, or open fires. Keep tents inside space; charcoal bins are provided. Nashville offers clubs, dining, music, museums within short distance.

::::::::::::::::::::::::::::::::::

SUNBELT CONFERENCE

::::::::::::::::::::::::::::::::::

ARKANSAS STATE UNIVERSITY
Indian Stadium
Jonesboro, Arkansas
(870) 972-3930

RVs park in lots south of stadium, starting Friday night; can stay till Sunday. Ten RV spots have hookups, $15 per day. No alcohol; visitors and home fans please clean up; don't stay past midnight. Area has many golf courses nearby.

UNIVERSITY OF IDAHO
Kibby Dome
Moscow, Idaho
(208) 885-6466 (208) 885-6424
(208) 885-0200

RVs park ahead of time; call -6424 extension to make arrangements. No alcohol allowed, but game ticket gets you into Alumni Area, where beer and food sold. Visit official tailgating events with food, music, and activities for kids. Leave immediately after game.

UNIVERSITY OF LOUISIANA AT LAFAYETTE

Cajun Field
Lafayette, Louisiana
(337) 482-5393

Cajun Field is off campus, but parking is within walking distance. Reserved RV and tailgating areas are for season ticket holders. Visitors do have a large first-come, first-served parking area. No glass containers, open fires, four-wheelers or motorcycles. Otherwise, come and have fun.

UNIVERSITY OF LOUISIANA AT MONROE

Malone Stadium
Monroe, Louisiana
(318) 342-3ULM

Most parking restricted; some lots for visitors to tailgate. RVs may come Thursday evening. Remember, keep inside your space. Try real Cajun cooking. Mmmm, good!

MIDDLE TENNESSEE STATE UNIVERSITY

Johnny "Red" Floyd Stadium
Murfreesboro, Tennessee
(615) 898-2210

RVs park the night before. There are parking lots, grass lots, parking on local streets, all within walking distance. No alcohol on campus; leave by Sunday night. Visit Hillbilly Hilton—serious tailgaters with huge grills feeding anyone within reach. Activities for kids.

NEW MEXICO STATE UNIVERSITY

Aggie Memorial Stadium
Las Cruces, New Mexico
(505) 646-2569

All tailgating done in single large, unpaved lot east of stadium. Visiting RVs may arrive a day early. No kegs allowed; keep alcohol in cups. Indulge in real Mexican food.

University of North Texas

Fouts Field
Denton, Texas
(940) 565-2527
(940) 369-7643

Visiting RVs park early if you call ahead. Tailgaters stay until midnight. No glass containers; don't drive stakes into ground for tents; please clean up afterward. Practice field has music, fun, kid stuff—just don't park there.

Troy State University

Movie Gallery Veterans Stadium
Troy, Alabama
(877) 878-9467

All campus parking reserved for donors, season ticket holders. One RV lot on campus without hookups for visitors, anyone. Parking available in town for various fees. RVs should leave Sunday afternoon. No kegs or glass containers; keep drinks in cups.

WESTERN ATHLETIC CONFERENCE

Boise State University

Bronco Stadium
Boise, Idaho
(208) 426-4737
(208) 426-3560

No specific lots for tailgating visitors. Visiting RVs or cars can park on street or find a space on campus, first-come, first-served basis. RVs call -3560 number for parking pass. Parking on the street can be done before game day. No open containers of alcohol.

California State University

Bulldog Stadium
Fresno, California
(559) 278-4167

RVs park in specific lots or on grass if you call ahead. Alcohol permitted only in two college-owned tailgating areas; other areas are state property. Tents must be 10 x 10 feet or smaller; stay inside your space.

UNIVERSITY OF HAWAII AT MANOA

Aloha Stadium
Honolulu, Hawaii
(808) 486-9500
www.alohastadium.hawaii.gov

Tailgating in specific lots available on first-come, first-served basis. Don't tailgate in other stadium lots. No reserving or saving parking spots; no dumping coals, pegging tents, or throwing balls or Frisbees in parking area.

LOUISIANA TECH UNIVERSITY

Jon Aillet Stadium
Ruston, Louisiana
(318) 257-4111

Park your car or RV; bring everything to specified tailgating picnic areas. RVs have specific lots for parking; can arrive 48 hours before game. No alcohol; stay within your space. Visit Tailgate Alley; enjoy the carnival atmosphere with music and food.

UNIVERSITY OF NEVADA

Mackay Stadium
Reno, Nevada
(775) 784-6900 ext. 293

Parking is free, woohoo! But there is tent rental fee. RVs park Friday after 6 p.m. and stay until 6 p.m. Sunday. No selling merchandise, food, or other items. Otherwise, have a blast; don't miss the big cooking competition. You can kayak downtown, too!

RICE UNIVERSITY

Rice Stadium
Houston, Texas
(713) 348-6930

Tailgaters park in Stadium Lot next to stadium, no charge. No overnight parking; come at 9 a.m. game day instead. No glass bottles; kegs okay, but must be registered with police. At afternoon games stay all day; evening games leave by 11 p.m.

SAN JOSÉ STATE UNIVERSITY

Spartan Stadium
San José, California
(408) 924-7589

RVs, buses call ahead to reserve spaces. No reserved pass; you'll be charged by number of spaces you take. No overnight parking. No alcohol after kickoff time.

SOUTHERN METHODIST UNIVERSITY

Gerald J. Ford Stadium
Dallas, Texas
(214) 768-2582

Campus lots reserved for season ticket holders; few spaces left for visitors. Most visitors park downtown, use shuttles. Most tailgating done in grassy picnic area called Boulevard. Limited space, but maybe you'll get lucky. No gas grills allowed.

UNIVERSITY OF TEXAS AT EL PASO

Sun Bowl Stadium
El Paso, Texas
(915) 747-5481

Two free RV lots; arrive 8 a.m. Friday, but stay with RV. Parking available for cars; most parking off campus. People tailgate at cars; shuttles are available. One space per vehicle; keep within your space; no drinking in shuttles.

THE UNIVERSITY OF TULSA

Skelly Stadium
Tulsa, Oklahoma
(918) 631-2935
www.tulsahurricane.com

Visitor parking on north end of campus off 5th Street; short walk to stadium. RVs park night before; no hookups, but free. Stay in front or back of vehicle; keep tents 10 x 10 feet or smaller; no grilling during fire alerts. Porta-potties, trash service provided.

UTAH STATE UNIVERSITY

Romney Stadium
Logan, Utah
(435) 797-1860 Kevin Dustin

All parking within walking distance; can't park overnight. No alcohol or glass containers. Friendly atmosphere; Dutch ovens used for cooking everything from ribs to cobblers.

NATIONAL FOOTBALL LEAGUE STADIUMS

ARIZONA CARDINALS
Sun Devil Stadium
Tempe, Arizona
(602) 379-0102

Parking for RVs on north side of stadium. No restrictions on tailgating items. Visit Cardinals' official tailgate party, Big Red Rage, for food, music, interactive games, live radio broadcast.

ATLANTA FALCONS
Georgia Dome
Atlanta, Georgia
(404) 223-8000 office
(404) 223-8444 operations

RVs park in yellow lot on corner of Simpson and Northside Drive. Most lots have no restrictions; no overnight parking. MARTA system carries people to game from around town.

The pregame party called Falcon's Landing has food, entertainment for free. Get here early; Atlanta's traffic is challenging.

BALTIMORE RAVENS
M&T Bank Stadium
Baltimore, Maryland
(410) 261-RAVE

There are 13 on-site lots at stadium controlled by Maryland Stadium Authority. Tailgating is allowed on all on-site lots. Due to limited space, on-site parking sold by permit only. Visit Raven's Walk for pregame fun, various sponsored activities. You will be frisked upon entering stadium. Really.

BUFFALO BILLS
Ralph Wilson Stadium
Orchard Park, New York
(716) 648-1800
(877) BB-TICKS

All parking surrounds stadium; overnight parking available $5 extra. Depending on availability, extra spaces may be purchased; no saving spaces for pals. Go to team's clubhouse for Tops' Gameday Experience, free with ticket; lots of cool stuff for all ages.

CAROLINA PANTHERS

Bank of America Stadium
Charlotte, North Carolina
(704) 358-7000

All parking is within a half-mile radius of stadium. Tailgate anywhere but parking decks; no overnight parking. Go to Cat Walk and Fun Zone for free pregame festivities.

CHICAGO BEARS

New Soldier Field
Chicago, Illinois
(847) 615-BEAR ticket office
(888) 79-BEARS fan services
(312) 583-9153 parking hotline
www.chicagobears.com

RVs, bigger vehicles park in Adler Planetarium on first-come, first-served basis. No overnight parking. No alcohol, ad banners, or displays; no political campaigning or protesting, tents, canopies, tethered blimps, balloons, oversized inflatables, weapons, fireworks, disorderly conduct, saving spaces, or in/out privileges; stay inside your space. Park in East Monroe Street or Millennium Park garages to use free stadium shuttle.

CINCINNATI BENGALS

Paul Brown Stadium
Cincinnati, Ohio
(513) 455-4800
(513) 946-8100 Central Parking

Parking available for RVs, larger vehicles, cars at various pricing. No overnight parking, parking's not cheap. Single-game lots available north of Third Street. Stay past 1 a.m., you're towed. No items restricted; prefer charcoal grills. Be prepared to use public transportation; visit Jungle Zone for pregame fun. Try the chili, too.

CLEVELAND BROWNS

Cleveland Browns Stadium
Cleveland, Ohio
(216) 367-7912 AMPCO Parking
(216) 664-2711 City Parking

Stadium doesn't offer parking. Best bet, nearby Port of Cleveland parking lot. Can prepay through AMPCO Parking. RVs can't park in garages; can park in open lots day before until morning after game. No open alcohol containers. Visit Buzzard Barking Lot for pregame fun.

DALLAS COWBOYS

Texas Stadium
Dallas, Texas
(972) 785-4000

Tailgating allowed in all Texas Stadium parking lots. Occupy as many spaces as you've got parking passes for. If bringing grill on trailer, buy additional spot for trailer. Ash cans, trash cans located throughout parking lots. Buses, shuttles available. Pre- and postgame party at The Corral tent, outside Gate 8. Fee is $3 with game ticket.

DENVER BRONCOS

Invesco Field at Mile High
Denver, Colorado
(720) 258-3000 parking information

Single game parking in southwest corner of stadium; $30 per space, first-come, first-served. RVs will likely use two spaces. Stadium has shuttles for elderly, disabled. No glass bottles, kegs, open fires, saving spaces, unauthorized vehicles, or blocking pedestrian access. No advertising, promoting, or selling anything without permission. Coal disposal bins provided. Broncos host tailgating contests with themes for different games.

DETROIT LIONS

Ford Field
Detroit, Michigan
(800) 616-ROAR
(313) 831-5236 Handy, Mobile
(586) 784-1005 Park Right
(313) 832-8154 Eastern Market

All public parking handled by private companies. Each has own rules, which differ. The Lions' Web site recommends Eastern Market, as there's a shuttle. Get spaces in advance from city's Parking Department.. More info at www.ci.detroit.mi.us/municipalpark/EasternMarket Tailgating2004.htm.

GREEN BAY PACKERS

Lambeau Field
Green Bay, Wisconsin
(920) 405-1121
(800) 895-0071 parking information

RVs can't park at stadium. Overnight RV parking for $60, three blocks away. RV day-only lot is $50, located across street from stadium. Most lots have coal disposal bins. Keep everything inside your space. Some downtown lots will sell an extra space; some won't. Pregame parties available across town; some charge small fee. This is bratwurst country.

HOUSTON TEXANS

Reliant Stadium
Houston, Texas
(832) 667-2000

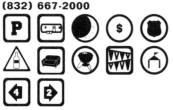

Stadium parking for season ticket holders. City parking within walking distance; cost varies; no parking overnight. Put away all tailgating items before entering game. No oversized balloons allowed; no alcohol before 10 a.m. Sunday.

INDIANAPOLIS COLTS

RCA Dome
Indianapolis, Indiana
(317) 636-8552
(317) 262-3400 RCA Dome

Tailgating available in South Lot, located immediately south of RCA Dome. You will be directed to parking spot. Hookups available for RVs; no night-before parking, but can leave day after. No open fires. Loads of pregame fun at C. P. Morgan Competition Center.

JACKSONVILLE JAGUARS

Alltel Stadium
Jacksonville, Florida
(904) 633-2000

Few stadium spaces for visitors; park in city and take shuttles. All must call to reserve a spot. A parking pass will be mailed to you. RVs have two lots; call ahead to get space; no overnight parking. Call (904) 353-1126 to reserve spot in the Tailgate Lot, for serious tailgaters. More expensive. No open fires. Visit Pepsi Plaza for pregame blast.

KANSAS CITY CHIEFS

Arrowhead Stadium
Kansas City, Missouri
(816) 920-4382

Parking close to stadium; shuttles available but unnecessary. Can't buy extra spaces, but there are grass areas for use. Tailgate in front of or behind vehicle; parking passes for vehicles, not trailers or tables.

MIAMI DOLPHINS

Pro Player Stadium
Miami, Florida
(305) 623-6000

Visitor parking is close to stadium; attendants will help you park. RVs have designated spots. No tents in the grass, saving spaces, kegs, or glass. Parking is first-come, first-served. The weather is usually great; visit South Beach and enjoy Miami nightlife, too.

MINNESOTA VIKINGS

Metrodome
Minneapolis, Minnesota
(612) 338-4537

In 2004 all tailgating moved to Rapid Park, behind Target Center. No overnight parking; no open fires. Unwise to wear Packers colors unless you want to get razzed. Local food specialty fried asparagus. Minneapolis offers much—go exploring!

NEW ENGLAND PATRIOTS

Gillette Stadium
Foxborough, Massachusetts
(508) 543-1776

Parking close; no shuttle needed. RVs have specific area; RV $125, cars $35, buses $200. Arrive early to get good spaces. RVs enter at P10, limos at P2 or P6, buses or disabled at P5 or P6. Check www.gillettestadium.com for prohibited item updates.

NEW ORLEANS SAINTS

Louisiana Superdome
New Orleans, Louisiana
(504) 587-3805

All cars park in attached garages, RVs in open lot. No personal tailgating allowed, even RVs. There's an official tailgate bash on garage rooftops, called Plaza Level. Quite the party. All current policies are up for review, so call ahead. Worst case, you're in New Orleans—how cool is that?

New York Giants
New York Jets

Giants Stadium
New York, New York
(201) 460-4187

Both teams use Giants Stadium. Parking surrounds stadium. If full, buses available on game day, running between stadium and Port Authority Bus Terminal, $7 round trip. No grilling on sidewalks or next to buildings; no open fires, ball playing, or Frisbee tossing. No overnight parking; dispose of charcoal safely. New arrivals, check your space for charcoal! Giants don't host any parties; Jets have four Oasis stations with different themes, alumni, gear, and more. Each has beer garden, seats 250, sells food. Check out the deluxe portable bathrooms. Very swank!

Oakland Raiders

Network Associates Coliseum
Oakland, California
(510) 615-1888

Gates open 5 a.m. No overnight parking in stadium lots; many do so across street a day or more before game. No glass containers; no open fires. Stadium serious about banned items. Enjoy whole pig and barbecue. San Francisco is 15 minutes away by train.

Philadelphia Eagles

Lincoln Financial Field
Philadelphia, Pennsylvania
(215) 339-6757

All parking within three-block radius around stadium. No shuttles, but subway is close by, if you come from downtown. RVs pay for number of spots used; no parking overnight; stay within space. No tailgating north of Pattison Ave. Visit Eagles Ultimate Tailgate Party; you'll need a ticket.

Pittsburgh Steelers

Heinz Field
Pittsburgh, Pennsylvania
(412) 323-4455 Alco Parking

Lots open 5 hours before game; parking $25–$35 per space. Large RVs might need four spaces; budget for it. Downtown garages only $5, but no grilling. No overnight parking or tents; one space per vehicle. You must take home whatever furniture you bring. Postgame activities in Lot 2; visit Cope's Cabaña.

San Diego Chargers

Qualcomm Stadium
San Diego, California
(619) 641-3100
(619) 281-6316

Parking lot surrounds stadium; first-come, first-served; opens 6 a.m. game day. Other parking is close by. Large parties can reserve space in certain lots. No overnight parking, throwing balls, scooters, or rollerblades; stay in your space; get a keg permit; get there before noon.

San Francisco 49ers

Monster Park
San Francisco, California
(415) 656-4949

All parking within main parking area next to stadium, all within walking distance. RVs have separate parking area; no overnight parking. Tailgate in front of or behind vehicle. One space per vehicle only. Must stay within your space! After game shop at Pier 39, eat in Chinatown, walk Golden Gate Bridge.

Seattle Seahawks

Qwest Field
Seattle, Washington
(206) 381-7816
www.seahawks.com

Parking limited due to location. Visitors park on private off-site lots, located at south end of stadium, within walking distance. No overnight parking; only propane grills allowed; no alcohol. Visit Touchdown City at south end of stadium for music, food, and more; free admission.

St. Louis Rams

Edward Jones Dome
St. Louis, Missouri
(800) 246-7267
(314) 241-7777 St. Louis Parking

All parking within one-mile radius. All are private lots; no stadium parking; shuttles provided. Game-day parking only; RVs charged for two spaces. Tailgating restrictions vary from lot to lot. Temperature always 72° Fahrenheit inside dome—enjoy.

TAMPA BAY BUCCANEERS

Raymond James Stadium
Tampa Bay, Florida
(813) 350-6500

Tailgating takes place around entire stadium. No shuttle service, just taxis. No overnight parking. Must stay within your space and no throwing footballs. Some hotels offer shuttles, some don't. Visit Coca-Cola Football Town USA, an interactive tailgate area with free admission. Local tailgating specialty is Cuban sandwiches—*muy bueno!*

TENNESSEE TITANS

The Coliseum
Nashville, Tennessee
(615) 565-4000

Tailgating takes place in stadium lots, within walking distance. RV parking for season ticket holders; no overnight parking. Shuttle service provided from downtown. No saving spaces, rowdy behavior, running, or jogging. Tailgate in front of or behind vehicle only. Stay inside your space; need permit for tents or canopies. Dispose of charcoal in coal bins.

WASHINGTON REDSKINS

FedEx Field
Washington, D.C.
(301) 276-6000

Tailgating permitted in all stadium parking lots. Tailgate in front of or behind your vehicle only; no buying extra spaces. Put out all flames and grills before game. Ash dumpsters available throughout lots. Shuttle service provided for cash lots. Stadium is 5 minutes from D.C.; visit National Museum of the American Indian while you're here.

NASCAR TRACKS

ATLANTA MOTOR SPEEDWAY
Hampton, Georgia
(770) 946-4211

NASCAR tailgating is an animal far different from its football-oriented cousins. Most of the "weekends" are at least four days long. Many RV parking passes mentioned below are actually season packages, which explains why some cost over $3,000 a whack. Some include race tickets; some don't. Many raceways are moving to a season-ticket-only format, with waiting lists over a year long. Call the track in question to find out about season versus weekend ticket availability.

Note: two locations were omitted from this list—Autodromo Hermanos Rodriguez and Nazareth Speedway. We excluded the Autodromo in this edition because it lies outside the United States; Nazareth Speedway does not appear to be operational at this time.

Parking close to track up to $75; farther away is free. Shuttle service available through www.vroomz.com—it provides shuttles for some travel packages. RVs can park up to a week before race day. No open fires, alcohol in family campgrounds, or golf carts.

BRISTOL MOTOR SPEEDWAY
Bristol, Tennessee
(423) 764-1161

RVs can arrive a week early, first-come, first-served basis, cars day of race. All should be gone end of race day. Shuttles provided for distant lots. Get tickets ahead of time; don't block roadways.

CALIFORNIA SPEEDWAY
Fontana, California
(800) 944-7223

All parking within walking distance. Parking in pit reserved for season ticket holders. There are 30,000 free parking spaces. RVs have designated lot; no overnight parking; no current prices available; call ahead. Parking still goes quickly; arrive early. One space per vehicle; no open fires. Any changes posted on race day.

CHICAGOLAND SPEEDWAY

Joliet, Illinois
(815) 727-7223

Cars park for free. Park on west side of Chicagoland Speedway; use shuttle. Several RV tailgater packages—from $200 for speedway campground to $2,450 for parking at Speedway Ridge. Overnight parking at Speedway Ridge and campground only. No open fires, unauthorized vehicles, or tent camping; one space per vehicle. Miller Lite sponsors free concert Friday evening of NASCAR Pole Day. Free shuttle from Joliet Union Station and back.

DARLINGTON RACEWAY

Darlington, South Carolina
(843) 395-8499

Overnight tent camping available. Reserved infield RV area with electric hookups; spaces $475 for weekend, includes two infield tickets. Additional infield tickets $100. Raceway has three reserved auto and van parking areas; call for prices. No large fires; stay within your space. Go to Darlington Stripe Zone to meet NASCAR personalities on race morning; first-come, first-served at $140. Leave at conclusion of event.

DAYTONA INTERNATIONAL SPEEDWAY

Daytona Beach, Florida
(386) 253-7223

Tailgating mostly done in track's infield. Shuttles available for lots 7 and 10. Lots A, 7, 10 park free. Lot 8 is remote RV parking, $200. Packages available for infield RV tailgating ranging from $315 to $900. No open fires; keep safety in mind when bringing items; keep everything calm.

DOVER INTERNATIONAL SPEEDWAY

Dover, Delaware
(800) 441-7223

Cars park on race day, $10. RV parking in lots 5, 8, 9, and 10 on first-come, first-served basis, $60; no infield parking. Lots 2 and 6 are reserved RV lots, $120 and $170 respectively. Only cash accepted! Cars pay $40 per day for infield parking, $60 overnight, not including tickets. Infield rules—no ground fires, tents, drunkenness, or temporary platforms. Safety above all else.

GATEWAY INTERNATIONAL SPEEDWAY

Madison, Illinois
(618) 875-7550

Overnight infield parking for RVs only. Most races, RV infield parking $15 to $75. NHRA Nationals or POWERade Drag Racing weekend RV parking $780 for Tier 1 with four weekend general admission tickets, $490 for Tier 2 with two tickets. Cars park for $15. No overnight parking in regular lots; stay within your space; no open fires.

HOMESTEAD-MIAMI SPEEDWAY

Homestead, Florida
(305) 230-7223

RV parking for two- or three-day weekend $195 in designated parks.

Free day parking. Only RVs park overnight. No gas grills or bonfires. Speedway is updating fan guidelines; call for updated information.

INDIANAPOLIS MOTOR SPEEDWAY

Indianapolis, Indiana
(317) 492-6535 parking safety
(317) 492-6700 ticket office

One-day parking for cars $20, RVs $40. Four-day pass $50 for cars, RVs $120–$150, premium RV lots $250. Tailgating done in North 40 lot, Turn 3, Turn 1 lots. Small portable grills allowed; no dumping charcoal or ground fires. Shelters must be 10 x 10 feet or smaller, secured to back of vehicle, and out of traffic. Rules and camping info at www.indianapolismotorspeedway.com/visitorinfo/regulations.php and www.indianapolismotorspeedway.com/visitorinfo/camping/.

INDIANAPOLIS RACEWAY PARK (IRP)

Indianapolis, Indiana
(317) 291-4090

Infield off limits. RVs park overnight at nearby campground, not track. During 60th Annual Night Before the 500, buses run to and from Indianapolis Motor Speedway.

More info to be added during 2005; check Web site. No open fires, no glass, no golf carts.

INFINEON RACEWAY

Sonoma, California

(800) 870-7223

Camping allowed in designated campgrounds, not parking lots. Trackside RV Terraces offer overnight and weekend parking. Prices range $35 to $1,500. Call ahead to get pass. General parking free. Camping rules: no open fires, barrel fires, or bad behavior. Pets must stay in campground. You're in wine country; go for winery tour while you're here.

KANSAS SPEEDWAY

Kansas City, Kansas

(913) 328-7223

Kansas Speedway's Reserved Infield, Motor Home Terrace, and Kansas Reserved Campground allow overnight stays. Season pass only; 2005 sold out. Tailgating starts early in the morning; no open fires; don't bring food, drink, or large bags into stadium. No parking in pit; general parking free.

KENTUCKY SPEEDWAY

Sparta, Kentucky

(888) 652-RACE

Reserved RV camping at Turns 1 and 2 runs $175 to $250 depending on event. General RV camping available off-site $30; shuttle to race provided. When camping: no golf carts; one dog per vehicle kept on leash; no fireworks; quiet hours begin 11 p.m. Only service animals allowed in facility, i.e. dogs for blind, deaf, physically disabled. Get ticket to visit Anheuser Busch Party Zone.

LAS VEGAS MOTOR SPEEDWAY

Las Vegas, Nevada

(702) 632-8169

(800) 644-4444 ticket office

Traffic can be heavy; arrive early. No parking in pit. El Monte RV lot accessible from Gate 1, using Las Vegas Boulevard. Call ticket office for space availability. No open fires; one space per vehicle; no external speakers; no tents or awnings. For NASCAR events, 5-day RV parking $199 general lot; for Motorhome Hill up to $3,100.

LOWE'S MOTOR SPEEDWAY

Concord, North Carolina
(770) 455-3209
(800) 455-FANS ticket office

RVs choose between general camping $75 per week or track's Fleetwood Campground with electric, water, sewer hookups, up to $525 per week. Keep fires contained; no fire pits; emphasis on safe, considerate behavior. Shuttles, trams available.

MANSFIELD MOTORSPORTS SPEEDWAY

Mansfield, Ohio
(419) 525-7223 Chris

RV parking $40 for four-day NASCAR weekend. Space limited; reservations on first-come, first-served basis. RV owners reserve adjoining sites by sending in forms together, with payments. All camping primitive; open fires in fire rings only; don't use 15-foot space between units. Reserved RV parking for season ticket holders runs $200 to $300.

MARTINSVILLE SPEEDWAY

Martinsville, Virginia
(726) 276-3151

RV, tent camping runs $20 to $40, depending on event. Site's dry; water and dumps available. Fee is for entire stay, not per night. Keep all wood fires contained, off of ground; no bikes or four-wheelers; keep within your space.

MEMPHIS MOTORSPORTS PARK

Memphis, Tennessee
(901) 358-7223

RV parking opens Thursday of race week. Fee $25 per day, $60 for four-day weekend on first-come, first-served basis. On NASCAR weekends, limited number of trackside RV spaces available at Turn 4. Fee is $350 for NCTS weekend, $500 for NBS weekend; both packages include four reserved seats in Grandstand G (start/finish line).

MICHIGAN INTERNATIONAL SPEEDWAY

Brooklyn, Michigan

(800) 354-1010

RV campsites start at $125 for remote sites, topping out at $400 for Turn 2 spaces with hookups. Fees cover several days' stay, depending on event. No glass, large coolers, large fires, golf carts, or drunk or disorderly conduct; can't rope off area.

MILWAUKEE MILE

West Allis, Wisconsin

(414) 266-7035 camping

Tailgating in fairgrounds parking areas $5, infield $10. Overnight RV parking available at State Fair RV Park; rates for NASCAR events $33 per night, electric only; or $44 with full-service hookup. Requires two- or three-night stay. Reservations needed for auto-racing weekends; call camping number above. No bonfires or tents.

NASHVILLE SUPERSPEEDWAY

Gladeville, Tennessee

(866) 722-3849

Day RV parking free. Overnight RV parking $30 weekend. Reserved RV parking limited; call ahead. Season RV parking for Ridge $770, for weekend $270, for Bluff $675 and $245. All include two race passes per event. No tent camping, pets, ground fires, hard liquor, or glass bottles. No small motorized vehicles; bikes okay. Safe, courteous behavior strongly encouraged.

NEW HAMPSHIRE INTERNATIONAL SPEEDWAY

Louden, New Hampshire

(603) 783-4931

RVs and campers park in designated campground. Fee is $100 per event weekend before July 1, 2005; afterward $125. No hookups or dump sites. No tents or open fires; one spot per RV/camper. Be prepared for cold weather, even in summer.

Phoenix International Raceway

Avondale, Arizona

(602) 252-2227

Reserved RV spaces with tow pass, $150. Reserved RV infield parking from $1,545 to $3,315 limited, call eight or nine months ahead to get space. General RV spaces $40 first-come, first-served. No roping off or saving spaces. Keep fires self-contained; weather may prohibit fires; no motorized carts. Child ID bracelets available.

Pikes Peak International Raceway

Fountain, Colorado

(888) 306-7223

RV parking runs $50 for weekend or overnight, to $1,050 for trackside season pass. No hookups available. Permits must be displayed. No ground fires; gas grills only. Shuttles available.

Pocono Raceway

Long Pond, Pennsylvania

(800) RACEWAY (722-3929)

RV fees range from single-day $40 per person on infield, to $500 trackside parking Thursday to Sunday. Call ahead for spaces. There are no hookups or dumpsites. No tent camping, pets, ground fires, unauthorized vehicles, amplified music, or fireworks.

Richmond International Raceway

Richmond, Virginia

(804) 345-7223

There's a 3- to 5-year wait for RV lots with no hookups, $175. With hookups, a 12- to 15-year wait, $250. Cars park free, but leave by midnight. All tailgating must be done directly in front of or behind vehicle. Most races sell out immediately—call fast!

TALLADEGA SUPERSPEEDWAY

Talladega, Alabama

(256) 362-7223

General RV parking in Red, Green Zones, $325; add $75 for one tow-in vehicle. Several packages available for reserved RV infield spots, starting $420. Other reserved spots are Reserved Family Park, Allison Motorhome Ave., with fees from $250 to $1,550. Cars, vans, SUVs have sliding rates depending on length of stay, from $245 to $285. No saving spaces, tent camping, or bonfires. Emphasis on civil behavior. Keep site tidy.

TEXAS MOTOR SPEEDWAY

Fort Worth, Texas

(817) 215-8500

Millions of dollars were recently spent on parking and camping improvements. Huge selection of reserved and general spaces for RVs, tent camping, cars, but it still sells out quickly. Prices range from $50 to $2,000. Best bet—call or go to www.texasmotorspeedway.com and click on Visitor Info. No open fires or ATVs; respect quiet-time rule.

WATKINS GLEN INTERNATIONAL

Watkins Glen, New York

(866) 461-RACE (7223)

Prices vary according to event. Much overnight parking perennially sold; call ahead. Tailgate Zone is reserved infield parking section, $100. Other spots range from trackside $375 to $70 unreserved. No water fights, spotlights, or unauthorized vehicles; no tents/canopies during race.

WIN A BOWL GAME WEEKEND

sponsored by

You and a friend could be spending part of your holiday watching the SEC and Big Ten battle it out at the Gaylord Hotels Music City Bowl Presented By Bridgestone!

www.MusicCityBowl.com

To enter, just log on to www.theultimatetailgater.com and register to win!

Sweepstakes Winner Receives:

- Airfare for two to Nashville, TN
- Three days/two nights accommodations at the Gaylord Opryland Resort and Convention Center
- 2 tickets to the Battle of the Bands VIP Party
- 2 tickets to the Coaches Luncheon

- 2 tickets to the official pregame Tailgate Party (of course!)
- 2 pregame sideline passes
- 2 Club Level tickets to the game
- 1 parking pass
- 2 official Bowl merchandise packs
- 2 Music City souvenir goodie bags

This year's game is December 30, 2005. Sweepstakes trip dates are December 29–31, 2005.
See the following page or www.theultimatetailgater.com for complete details and Official Rules.

Official Rules

NO PURCHASE NECESSARY. To enter, log on to www.theultimatetailgater.com and complete the online entry form. If you do not have Internet access, you may write the required information on any size postcard accepted by the U.S. post office. Include your name, address, age, daytime and evening phone numbers with area code, and your e-mail address. Mail to: *The Ultimate Tailgater's Handbook Sweepstakes*, c/o Interactive Blvd, P.O. Box 121646, Nashville, TN 37212-1646. Multiple entries are not permitted. Interactive Blvd is not responsible for lost, late, damaged, or illegible entries. Entries must be received between July 1, 2005, and November 4, 2005. Judges will select a winner by a random drawing to be conducted on or about November 11, 2005; the judges' decision will be final. The prize winner will be notified by phone.

One Grand Prize—A trip for two to Nashville, Tennessee, for the Gaylord Hotels Music City Bowl Presented by Bridgestone including: two tickets to the Battle of the Bands VIP Party, two tickets to the Coaches' Luncheon, two tickets to the official pregame Tailgate Party, two pregame sideline passes, two Club Level tickets to the game, one parking pass, two official Bowl merchandise packs, and two Music City souvenir goodie bags. Includes roundtrip coach air travel from within the continental U.S. for the prize winner and one companion, two nights hotel accommodation (double occupancy) at the Gaylord Opryland Resort and Convention Center (Thursday and Friday, December 29 and 30, 2005).

Winner is responsible for transportation to the airport nearest their home with available flight service to Nashville, Tennessee, and for transportation in Nashville. A shuttle is provided by Gaylord Opryland Hotel from the airport to the hotel. Approximate retail value of the package is $2,000. This prize has no cash value and may not be redeemed for any cash prize.

General Rules—Open only to legal residents of the continental United States age 18 and over. Void where prohibited by law. Employees of 4964 Productions, LLC, Creative Access, Inc., Thomas Nelson Publishers, Nashville Sports Council, Nashville Area Chamber of Commerce, What a Trip, the American Tailgaters Association any other sweepstakes sponsor, their affiliates, subsidiaries, advertising or promotional agencies, and their immediate family members and/or those living in the same household as these persons are not eligible. No substitution or transfer of prize is permitted. All federal, state, and local taxes are the sole responsibility of the winner. All federal, state, and local laws apply. Potential winner and all travelers must submit an Affidavit of Eligibility/Release of Liability/Prize Acceptance Form within seven days of attempted notification. Noncompliance within this time period may result in disqualification and an alternate winner may be selected. Trip must be taken on dates specified by sponsor. Dates of return and departure are subject to change. Sponsor reserves the right to substitute a prize of equal or greater value. Winner consents that sponsors may use the winner's name, photograph, or other likeness, the winner's hometown and biographical information, statements concerning the contest entry, or sponsor's products without compensation for purposes of advertising, promotion, and merchandising, and grant all rights to edit or modify and publish and copyright it. The winner must also make himself or herself available to travel at the sponsor(s) expense for promotional purposes. By accepting the prize, winner agrees to hold sponsor(s), and their respective directors, officers, employees, and assigns, harmless against any and all claims and liability arising out of prize. Prize winners assume all liability for any injury or damage caused, or claimed to be caused, by participating in this promotion. Entrants agree to be bound by the Official Rules and the decisions of the judges. Odds of winning depend on the total number of entries received. For name of winner (available after November 30, 2005), log on to www.theultimatetailgater.com or send a separate stamped, self-addressed business-size envelope to: Winners, *The Ultimate Tailgater's Handbook Sweepstakes*, c/o Interactive Blvd, P.O. Box 121646, Nashville, TN 37212-1646.

This Sweepstakes is sponsored by Interactive Blvd, a division of 4964 Productions, LLC, and the American Tailgaters Association. Thomas Nelson Publishers, Rutledge Hill Press, and retail locations are not responsible for entry process, winner selection, or prize distribution in this sweepstakes.

CROSSWORD PUZZLE ANSWERS

NFL (pages 84–85)

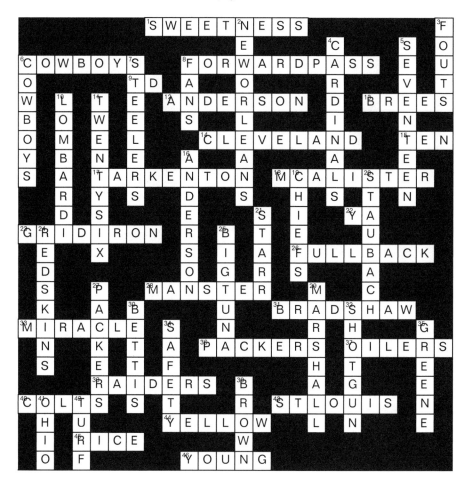

College Football (pages 86–87)

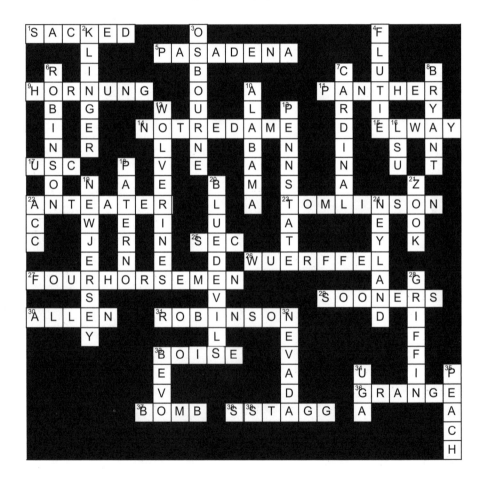

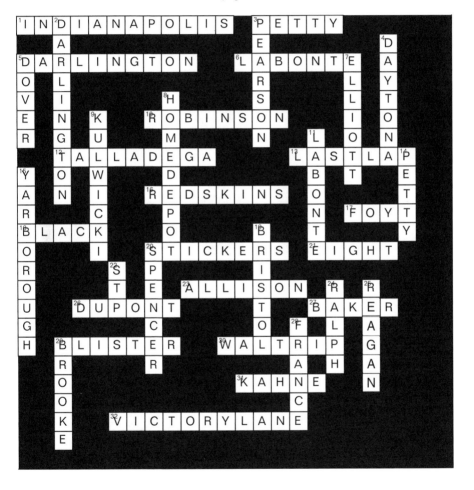

Across:

1. INDIANAPOLIS
3. PETTY
5. DARLINGTON
6. LABONTE
10. ROBINSON
12. TALLADEGA
13. LASTLAP
16. REDSKINS
17. FOYT
18. BLACK
20. STICKERS
21. EIGHT
23. ALLISON
26. DUPONT
27. BAKER
29. BLISTER
30. WALTRIP
31. KAHNE
32. VICTORYLANE